Instructor's Manual

READING AND THE WRITING PROCESS

SECOND EDITION

Susan Day
ILLINOIS STATE UNIVERSITY

Robert Funk
EASTERN ILLINOIS UNIVERSITY

Elizabeth McMahan
ILLINOIS STATE UNIVERSITY

MACMILLAN PUBLISHING COMPANY
NEW YORK

Macmillan Publishing Company
866 Third Avenue, New York, New York 10022

Macmillan Publishing Company is part of the
Maxwell Communications Group of Companies.

Maxwell Macmillan Canada, Inc.
1200 Eglinton Avenue East, Suite 200
Don Mills, Ontario M3C 3N1

ISBN   0-02-327902-8

Printing: 1 2 3 4 5 6 7 8   Year: 4 5 6 7 8 9 0 1 2 3

PREFACE

The instruction in the second edition of *READING AND THE WRITING PROCESS* is based on the premises that reading and writing go together and that students write better when they know how to read carefully and critically. This Instructor's Manual reflects our belief that a student-centered classroom provides the best environment for learning. We have found that peer involvement is invaluable in helping student writers to explore ideas, focus thoughts, develop drafts, and carry out revising and editing. We also consider class and small-group discussion the best methods for making crucial connections between reading and writing and thinking.

In this Instructor's Manual we provide commentary about the reading selections, guidance for implementing the writing assignments, and directions for using the instructional apparatus in the text. We frequently offer suggestions for employing a workshop approach with the various pedagogical activities in each chapter. We also provide suggested answers for the exercises and make recommendations for ways to individualize instruction and utilize additional readings.

We hope that you will enjoy teaching from *Reading and the Writing Process* and that your students will find the book both enlightening and enjoyable.

Susan Day
Robert Funk
Elizabeth McMahan

CONTENTS

ANTHOLOGY OF EXPRESSIVE WRITING

PART III   INFORMATIVE WRITING

ANTHOLOGY OF INFORMATIVE WRITING

PART IV   PERSUASIVE WRITING

ANTHOLOGY OF PERSUASIVE ESSAYS

PART V   RESEARCHED WRITING

HOW TO USE THE TEXT

General Contents

Part I, "Reading and Composing: An Overview," contains three chapters that explore and develop the connections between reading and writing.

> CHAPTER 1 is designed to help students become active readers. It also demonstrates the important role that writing plays in the improvement of reading skills.

> CHAPTER 2 introduces students to the main steps in the process of writing about essays. It provides concise instruction in generating ideas, planning a paper, developing material, and composing a first drafting.

> CHAPTER 3 examines rewriting. It offers advice on revising in stages and includes two versions of a revised student paper, along with the author's explanations of her revising procedures.

Part II, "Expressive Writing," contains three chapters that provide instruction in writing about feelings and personal experiences. These chapters are followed by an Anthology of Expressive Writing.

> CHAPTER 4 reviews the process of critical reading as it applies to expressive essays.

> CHAPTER 5 focuses on reading and writing narrative discourse.

> CHAPTER 6 explores ideas and techniques for developing a written voice.

Part III, "Informative Writing," contains three chapters that examine the principal features of expository writing. These chapters are followed by an Anthology of Informative Writing.

> CHAPTER 7 presents guidelines for collecting, evaluating, and reporting information.

> CHAPTER 8 focuses on organizational schemes for expository essays.

> CHAPTER 9 investigates techniques for developing the content of informative writing.

Part IV, "Persuasive Writing," consists of three chapters that examine strategies of persuasion, followed by an Anthology of Persuasive Essays.

CHAPTER 10 analyzes procedures for gaining the reader's respect and trust.

CHAPTER 11 focuses on the elements of constructing an argumentative essay.

CHAPTER 12 discusses methods for presenting a coherent argument.

Part V, "Researched Writing," contains a chapter on documented writing and a handbook for editing.

CHAPTER 13 gives detailed advice on using and documenting library sources, including an explanation of MLA and APA documentation styles and two sample papers.

CHAPTER 14 consists of 20 sections on the grammar and mechanics of standard written English. Each section presents a brief explanation of the key rules and provides 14 exercises for checking understanding. Answers for the exercises are provided in this manual.

The Basic Chapter Sequence

After the three introductory chapters of Part I, the remaining chapters (4-12) in parts II, III, and IV advance the connection between reading and writing. Each of these chapters follows a general sequence of reading, prewriting, writing, and rewriting.

The readings have been chosen to demonstrate effective writing strategies as well as to engage students' interests and provide them with ideas for their own writing. Students plan and develop an essay that proceeds from their analysis and understanding of the reading selection(s). The prewriting, planning, and revising activities change in each chapter, with the instruction and exercises correlated to the specific rhetorical focus of the chapter.

The reading and writing assignments begin with personal essays and move to exposition and persuasion. These assignments reflect tasks in academic writing and draw on real-world topics that should appeal to a wide range of students, including returning adults.

Setting a Schedule

If you are on a one-hour-period, three-day-a-week schedule (such as Monday, Wednesday,

Friday from 9 to 10), here is a schedule that you might use for covering a typical chapter in parts II, III, and IV:

Monday: Discuss primary reading (previously assigned), using the questions and activities provided. Introduce and discuss the writing assignment. Begin prewriting.

Wednesday: Legible draft brought in to class to work on. Peer response and rewriting.

Friday: Revised papers brought in. Do editing in groups or as a whole class. Collect papers. Assign primary reading for next class.

Monday: Return papers with brief comments. Discuss assigned reading and begin next essay.

And so on until you drop. . . . Actually, this schedule appears more breakneck than it is: the readings and student essays, especially at first, are not difficult, and we will suggest ways to vary the pattern and bring in other work, as needed. *Reading and the Writing Process* is a flexible book; it contains a lot of material that can be added or omitted as time and the needs of your students dictate.

Varying the Pattern

As you work your way through this text, you will discover ways to tailor the basic chapter sequence to your own teaching situation. We offer possibilities for varying the plan in the individual chapter sections of this manual. Here are some general suggestions to think about as you go:

● Adjust the length of the assignments. Many of the essays and revising projects can be simplified.

● Balance the in- and out-of-class work. The basic chapter sequence calls for quite a bit of in-class writing; but if your class time is limited, you may consider having students do more writing out of class--for example, answers to the questions about the readings, prewriting activities, peer responses, and rewriting exercises.

● If you have plenty of class time (some writing classes meet more than three times a week), then use some of the readings from the three anthologies to vary the pace and supplement the material in the chapters.

- Reconsider the amount of graded work. Can some assignments be graded *pass/fail* or *check/check-plus/check-minus*? Can you leave the essays ungraded and ask the students to choose several to revise for a grade at the middle or end of the course?

- Alter the chapter parameters. For example, spend less time on the reading and go right to the writing assignment. Or concentrate on the prewriting and planning and cut back on in-class revising.

- In the revising process, have students select the one suggestion that seems most productive or significant, and rewrite only the section that pertains to that suggestion. Have students turn in the complete first draft and the revised section; spend most of your evaluation time on the rewritten part.

- Do fewer chapters, and take more time for each topic or kind of writing. Think about selecting the chapters that seem most important to you, and use the anthologies of essays to augment the instruction.

- Organize the semester into two-week units, with the first week devoted to reading and discussion (using supplemental readings from the anthologies) and the second to writing (with drafting, peer review, and rewriting done in class).

- Have students collaborate on a writing assignment, giving you only one paper per group to respond to (instead of four or five).

Most importantly, don't lock yourself into a certain structure until you have tried several chapters. Hand out a detailed syllabus a chapter or two at a time. Keep looking at the variations and readjusting within the general framework until you find a system that works for you and your students.

Planning for the Semester

If you follow the weekly schedule given above, with three class periods for each chapter, you can work straight through this book at the rate of one chapter per week for 13 weeks. This is the length of a typical college semester (with an extra week or two for exams and other business). If such a pace is unrealistic, you can make some of the adjustments that we just described.

For a more deliberate program of study, we recommend spending an extra class period or two on each of the first three chapters and then selecting two chapters from each of the remaining parts to work on for the rest of the semester (that's a total of 9 chapters plus the research chapter). You may want to spend less time on expressive writing, for

4

example, and give more emphasis to persuasion and the research paper. Or skip the chapters on voice and credibility and spend more time on organization and developing content. A slower pace will also allow you to incorporate additional readings from the anthologies.

Using the Anthologies

The three collections of additional essays provide a variety of selections that can be used to substitute for the primary reading in a chapter or as supplements to the chapter readings. As you become familiar with the contents of this textbook, you will probably discover readings in the anthology that fit your own goals and your students' interests better than the ones we've chosen to use in a particular chapter.

You can also assign readings for students to compare and contrast--in terms of argument, style, ideas, and the like. The Comparative Study suggestions that accompany each selection in the anthologies will help you to correlate readings. Or just let the students do some extra reading on their own, and write about it in their journals.

A group of related essays can serve as the basis for a controlled research paper. Students won't have to go to the library; or they can begin by reading selections in the text and then supplement their research with interviews or library materials. The Thematic Table of Contents will assist you and your students in choosing a set of readings to use as sources for a documented paper.

Using the Handbook

The Handbook for Editing (Chapter 14) is intended to serve as a reference source. While it reviews all the essentials of English grammar, punctuation, and mechanics, its coverage is brief. It offers only a few examples on each point and the exercises are not extensive. It is not intended as a substitute for a standard book-length grammar.

Students will master the mechanics and structure of standard English more easily if they have the incentive to apply the rules to their own writing. For this reason, you should try to integrate the instruction and exercises of the Handbook with the revising and editing that students are doing on their essays. Assign particular sections to students based on their individual needs. Students can work on exercises independently or with a tutor, and you can check their work in conferences or ask them to hand in completed exercises for credit. If a problem seems widespread, you may want to have the entire class look at the appropriate section(s) in the Handbook and then review the material together.

5

ELEMENTS OF TEACHING THE COURSE

Getting Started

The first day of class can be difficult, especially since some students may not have their books yet. You'll need to be flexible, but you don't want to waste the first period. One of our colleagues begins each semester with a getting-acquainted activity. He tells the students that he's going to leave the room for ten minutes and that he wants them to learn one another's first names while he's gone. When he returns, he asks someone to introduce him to everyone in the class. (He makes it clear that no one will be shot if he or she misses a name.) Someone always volunteers, he says, and as the introductions are made, the teacher shakes each student's hand. He then asks for several more volunteers to go through the names (without the handshaking). This activity helps to break down inhibitions and sets a friendly tone for the beginning of the course.

Because it's important to get students writing from the start of the course, you might use a get-acquainted activity that involves writing. Pair students up and have them converse with each other for ten minutes or so. If you want, write these questions on the board for the pairs to use in their conversations:
1. What does everybody know about you?
2. Is there anything that very few people know about you? What is it?
3. What would you like your classmates to know about you?
Tell them to take notes, and give them five more minutes or so to write up a brief paragraph about their partner. Then ask them to read their paragraphs to the class--or collect the paragraphs and read them aloud to the class (disregarding errors, of course). At the end of the first class, you should give a specific assignment. For example:

Read the "Overview" and the first part of Chapter 1--through page 15. Be prepared to discuss what "active reading" is and what "prereading" involves, and also be ready to talk about your reactions to the essay "My Wood" by E. M. Forster.

If you want the students to do some writing for the next class, ask them to respond to Forster's essay in a paragraph or two about the effect that owning a valuable piece of property (such as a car or stereo) has had on them.

Using Journals

In the first chapter (p. 17), we suggest that students keep a record of their personal responses to the readings for this course. A journal is a excellent place for students to experience the process of writing. Journals don't involve the usual pressures associated with most college

6

writing assignments, and they provide a low-risk opportunity for student writers to pursue their ideas and explore their thoughts.

If you decide to assign journals, you have several ways to go about it. You can ask students to keep a reading journal in which they record reactions to and thoughts about the reading selections. These entries can then be used as a springboard for class discussions and as prewriting for the writing assignments. Journal entries might also be written in class during the last ten or fifteen minutes to get students ready for a reading assignment. You can provide cues for writing that promote close reading and encourage students to make connections with their own experiences. The Prereading Journal Ideas that accompany the anthology selections in this manual will give you some sense of the type of questions to use.

Many instructors collect and read their students' journals every week or so, although you can set several deadlines throughout the semester when you will pick up journals. You can stagger the deadlines, collecting journals from only certain students at any one time. You don't have to read and respond to every entry, but you need to make the journals seem worthwhile or the work will be slack. You can give bonus points for substantial entries or base a grade on a minimum length. We have found that assigning at least 10% of the semester grade to a journal and setting a minimum number of entries (e.g., three one-page entries per week) for a C works rather well. You can reward those students who write more and deduct from the grade of those who don't write enough.

Group Work and Peer Editing

In the text and in this manual we frequently suggest that students work in pairs or small groups for a variety of reasons: to compare responses to the readings, to generate ideas for writing, to make suggestions to one another for revising and improving their essays. Not all teachers are comfortable with using student groups, but the practice of having students work together has several significant advantages: 1) students develop a greater sense of audience; 2) they become more involved in the class; 3) the teacher doesn't have to do all the work of leading discussions and responding to essays.

We give tips about using group work in the individual chapter sections of this manual. Here are some general recommendations and points to consider:

1. Think carefully about whether you want students to stay with the same partner/group for most of the semester or change around. Stable groups promote more rapport and commitment, but they can grow stale.
2. Have students stay with the same partner for peer review of essays, but occasionally put pairs together or tell students to solicit a second (or even a third) opinion from another partner. If peer advice is contradictory, as it sometimes is, allow the student

7

to decide which suggestions to follow. Doing multiple peer responses will virtually assure that everyone gets some good advice. And sorting out the bad feedback from the good provides valuable learning experience.

3. Larger groups of 5 to 7 work well for discussions of readings, prewriting activities, and rewriting. The make-up of these groups can be changed frequently.

4. Provide plenty of structure for the groups, especially in the early stages. You can provide specific questions to consider in reviewing an essay, discuss the questions with the whole class, model sample responses, and ask for other questions to add to the list.

5. Peer review works better when you collect the written responses (done in full sentences) and evaluate them (with check, plus, or minus) along with the revisions. We also tell students that peer review is a *required* part of completing the writing assignment: no peer review, no grade.

6. Two or three times during the semester, collect brief written reports on how well the group work is going. Ask students to reflect on what they've learned from giving and getting peer feedback on their writing.

7. After two or three weeks, sit in on groups/pairs and, if necessary, give suggestions on how to improve their interactions.

8. Above all, be flexible and patient. Group work won't succeed if you don't give it a chance to develop.

Responding to Student Writing

Responding to student papers is one of the hardest parts of a writing teacher's job, but it's an essential one. You have to decide when to respond and what form your responses will take. The following chart relates possible responses and roles to the stages of the writing process; it may help clarify your goals as a reader and evaluator of student writing:

STAGE:	PREWRITING	DRAFTING	REVISION	COMPLETION
Writer's focus:	Ideas	Fluency	Clarity	Correctness
Kind of assessment:	Observing	Responding	Evaluating	Grading
Teacher's roles:	Listener/ encourager	Encourager/ coach	Editor/ expert	Expert/ judge
Goal of feedback:	Probing for interest	Helping, suggesting	Inquiring, evaluating	Judging, grading

[Adapted from Steven Zemelman and Harvey Daniels, *A Community of Writers*, Heinemann, 1988: 223]

Here are some suggestions about responding to student writing that you may find helpful:

1. While students are doing in-class writing, take a look at as many papers as you can and give some instant feedback. Also, hold individual conferences so that you can make your comments in person, one-on-one. A few minutes of personal discussion about a paper can often be more helpful than a page of written comments.
2. Let your students help each other. Much of the practical evaluation of a draft (determining if it meets the assignment, makes sense, sticks to the topic, needs more development, etc.) can be addressed in peer review sessions.
3. Read a revised paper through once in its entirety before you mark anything, even minor mechanical errors. This will allow you to assess the major strengths and weaknesses and target your responses.
4. Don't comment on everything. Focus your responses by setting some priorities for each paper. For instance, if the assignment stresses organization and the use of details, then try to restrict your comments to these features. There's a limit on how much feedback a student writer can take in and profit from.
5. Always provide some positive feedback: "These are good details"; "That's a clear topic sentence"; "I like your use of humor here"; "This paper is much better than the last one"; "I can see that you're on the right track"; etc. Many students lack confidence in their writing abilities and benefit from praise and encouragement.
6. Also set priorities about errors. Decide which ones cause the most problems and limit yourself to marking those. Emphasize that although you're marking only key errors, students are still responsible for trying to eliminate all the errors from their writing.
7. Maintain an objective, supportive tone in your comments. Students sometimes confuse criticism of their writing with personal criticism; a snide remark or a joke could damage your rapport.
8. Remember that you don't have to read and mark everything your students write. Your goal is to get students to take responsibility for their own development and improvement as writers.

9

BIBLIOGRAPHY OF USEFUL SOURCES

The following books and articles will explain and amplify the pedagogical principles and methods that inform *Reading and the Writing Process* and this manual.

READING AND WRITING

Birnbaum, June Cannell. "Reflective Thought: The Connection Between Reading and Writing." *Convergences: Transactions in Reading and Writing*. Ed. Bruce T. Petersen. Urbana: NCTE, 1986. 30-45.

Hairston, Maxine. "Using Nonfiction Literature in the Composition Classroom." *Convergences: Transactions in Reading and Writing*. Ed. Bruce T. Petersen. Urbana: NCTE, 1986. 179-88.

Peters, John. *The Elements of Critical Reading*. New York: Macmillan, 1991.

Reagan, Sally Barr. "Teaching Reading in the Writing Classroom." *Journal of Teaching Writing* 5 (1986): 177-85.

Wiener, Harvey S. "Inference: Perspectives on Literacy for Basic Skills Students." *Journal of Basic Writing* 11:1 (Spring 1992): 16-33.

INVENTION

Belanoff, Pat, Peter Elbow, and Sheryl Fontaine, eds. *Nothing Begins with N: New Investigations of Freewriting*. Carbondale: Southern Illinois UP, 1991.

Elbow, Peter. "The Loop Writing Process." *Writing with Power*. New York: Oxford UP, 1981. 59-77.

Larson, Richard. "Discovery Through Questioning: A Plan for Teaching Rhetorical Invention." *College English* 30.7 (Nov. 1968): 126-34.

Schneck, Mary Jane. "Writing Right Off: Strategies for Invention." *Training the New Teacher of College Composition*. Ed. Charles W. Bridges. Urbana: NCTE, 1986. 84-94.

Simpson, Jeanne H. *The Elements of Invention*. New York: Macmillan, 1990.

Washington, Eugene. "WH-Questions in Teaching Composition." *College Composition and Communication* 28.1 (Feb. 1977): 54-56.

REVISION

Harris, Muriel. "Composing Behaviors of One- and Multi-Draft Writers." *College English* 51.2 (Feb. 1989): 174-91.

Huff, Roland K. "Teaching Revision: A Model of the Drafting Process." *College English* 45.8 (Dec. 1983): 800-16.

Lindemann, Erika. "Teaching Rewriting." *A Rhetoric for Writing Teachers*. 2nd ed. New York: Oxford UP, 1987. 171-88.

Murray, Donald. "Teaching the Motivating Force of Revision." *Learning by Teaching*. Upper Montclair, NJ: Boynton/Cook, 1982.

Schwartz, Mimi. "Revision Profiles: Patterns and Implications." *College English* 45.6 (Oct. 1983): 549-58.

Sommers, Nancy. "Revision Strategies of Student Writers and Experienced Adult Writers." *College Composition and Communication* 31.4 (Dec. 1980): 378-88.

GROUP WORK/PEER REVIEW

George, Diana. "Working with Peer Groups in Composition Class." *College Composition and Communication* 35.3 (Oct. 1984): 320-26.

Gere, Anne Ruggles. *Writing Groups: History, Theory, and Implications*. Carbondale: Southern Illinois UP, 1987.

Grimm, Nancy. "Improving Students' Responses to Their Peers' Essays." *College Composition and Communication* 37 (1986): 91-94.

Holt, Mara. "The Value of Written Peer Criticism." *College Composition and Communication* 43.3 (Oct. 1992): 384-92.

Lapidus-Saltz, Wendy. "The Effective Feedback Script: A Peer Response Procedure." *The Writing Instructor* 1 (Fall 1981): 19-25.

Spear, Karen. *Sharing Writing: Peer Response Groups in English Classes*. Portsmouth, NH: Heinemann, 1988.

Wiener, Harvey S. "Collaborative Learning in the Classroom: A Guide to Evaluation." *College English* 48.1 (Jan. 1986): 52-61.

RESPONSE AND EVALUATION

Connors, Robert J., and Andrea A. Lunsford. "Teachers' Rhetorical Comments on Student Papers." *College Composition and Communication* 44.2 (May 1993): 200-23.

Elbow, Peter. "Ranking, Evaluating, and Liking: Sorting Out Three Forms of Judgment." *College English* 55.2 (Feb. 1993): 187-206.

Hairston, Maxine. "On Not Being a Composition Slave." *Training the New Teacher of College Composition*.5 Ed. Charles W. Bridges. Urbana: NCTE, 1986. 117-24.

Haswell, Richard H. "Minimal Marking." *College English* 45.6 (Oct. 1983): 600-04.

Heller, Dana A. "Silencing the Soundtrack: An Alternative to Marginal Comments." *College Composition and Communication* 40.2 (May 1989): 210-215

Larson, Richard L. "Making Assignments, Judging Writing, and Annotating Papers: Some Suggestions." *Training the New Teacher of College Composition*. Ed. Charles W. Bridges. Urbana: NCTE, 1986. 109-16.

Lynch, Denise. "Easing the Process: A Strategy for Evaluating Composition." *College Composition and Communication* 33.3 (Oct. 1982): 310-14.

Sommers, Nancy. "Responding to Student Writing." *College Composition and Communication* 33.2 (May 1982): 148-56.

GRAMMAR AND ERROR

Funk, Robert W., Elizabeth McMahan, and Susan Day. *The Elements of Grammar for Writers*. New York: Macmillan, 1991.

Harris, Muriel, and Katherine E. Rowan. "Explaining Grammatical Concepts." *Journal of Basic Writing* 8.2 (Fall 1989): 21-41.

Hartwell, Patrick. "Grammar, Grammars, and the Teaching of Grammar." *College English* 47.2 (Feb. 1985): 105-27.

Noguchi, Rei R. *Grammar and the Teaching of Writing: Limits and Possibilities*. Urbana: NCTE, 1991.

Sedgwick, Ellery. "Alternatives to Teaching Formal, Analytical Grammar." *Journal of Developmental Education* 12.3 (Spring 1989): 8-10, 12, 14, 20.

Shaughnessy, Mina P. *Errors and Expectations: A Guide for the Teacher of Basic Writing*. New York: Oxford UP, 1977.

JOURNALS

Berthoff, Anne E. *Forming/Thinking/Writing: The Composing Imagination*. Rochelle Park, NJ: Hayden, 1978.

Fulwiler, Toby, ed. *The Journal Book*. Portsmouth: Heinemann, 1987.

Huff, Roland, and Charles R. Kline, Jr. *A Contemporary Writing Curriculum: Rehearsing, Composing, and Valuing*. New York: Columbia UP, 1987. 1-51.

Prices, Gayle. "A Case for a Modern Commonplace Book." *College Composition and Communication* 31.2 (May 1980): 175-82.

Whitehall, Sharon. "Using the Journal for Discovery: Two Devices." *College Composition and Communication* 38.4 (Dec. 1987): 472-74.

RESEARCH PAPERS

Duke, Charles R. "Re: Search Writing." *Teaching English in the Two-Year College* 13 (Feb. 1986): 35-41

Larson, Richard L. "The 'Research Paper' in the Writing Course: A Non-Form of Writing." *College English* 44.8 (Dec. 1981): 811-16.

Jeske, Jeff. "Borrowing from the Sciences: A Model for the Freshman Research Paper." *The Writing Instructor* 6 (Winter 1987): 62-67.

McCartney, Robert. "The Cumulative Research Paper." *Teaching English in the Two-Year College* 12 (1985): 198-202.

Quantic, Diane. "Insights into the Research Process from Student Logs." *Journal of Teaching Writing* 5 (Fall 1986): 211-25.

Schmersahl, Carmen B. "Teaching Library Research: Process, Not Product." *Journal of Teaching Writing* 6 (1987): 231-38.

Williams, Nancy. "Research as a Process: A Transactional Approach." *Journal of Teaching Writing* 7 (1988): 193-204.

PART ONE

READING AND COMPOSING: AN OVERVIEW (p. 1)

This brief introduction to the text is intended to convince students of the importance of reading in learning to write well. Reading theorist Frank Smith asserts that there is no way we can learn anything as complex, as intricate, as tricky, as difficult as the composing process--except by "learning to write from what we read." Writing specialists agree. All acknowledge that reading and writing are related in various significant ways. Everyone we know who has become a proficient writer has also been an extensive reader.

You can help your students in their efforts to become good writers by assigning lots of outside reading. There are three essay anthologies included in this text to provide plenty of reading material: an Anthology of Expressive Writing, an Anthology of Informative Writing, and an Anthology of Persuasive Writing. Have your students read them.

Chapter 1

READING FOR WRITING (p.5)

This chapter focuses on the need to become an active reader and explains to students how to get involved with the text on the page. The aim is to turn them into willing and habitual readers.

Becoming an Active Reader (p. 6)

You will want to tell your students at the first class meeting to read this first chapter before coming to class for the second meeting. Be sure that they understand that they are to mark the text of Forster's "My Wood," as directed in section entitled "Practicing Active Reading."

Prereading (p. 6)

The term *prereading* can refer to a number of activities that readers perform before actually starting in on a text, such things as prediction and surveying (as explained in this section).

But prereading exercises can also be used to by an instructor to provide clues to understanding a difficult essay or to put students in a receptive mood for reading a controversial essay--one whose ideas they might reject if unprepared to consider them objectively. You will find throughout this text, as well as in the Instructor's Manual, a number of these sort of prereading assignments. They are perfect for journal writing. You can ask for volunteers to read their prereading responses from their journals as you begin the discussion of the essay. But whether or not you spend class time on the prereading suggestions, you should always assign them for the insights they may stimulate and the additional (ungraded) writing practice they provide.

Marking a Text (p. 7)

Probably most of your students have engaged in little or no interaction with the text before beginning this course. They are so firmly taught in public school not to deface their textbooks, that you will need to be equally firm about the need now to write in the book.

As you are assigning this chapter during the first class meeting, hold up your book and show them Fig. 1-1, which illustrates a text marked by an active reader. Or, better yet, show them some book of your own in which you have underlined, starred major points, and written comments in the margins. But make it clear to them that they should do their own marking of Forster's essay before looking to see how another reader marked it in Fig. 1-1.

Explain that naturally everyone will not mark a passage in the same way, but make it clear that readers should mark with a purpose in mind--to underline a major point, to mark a word that is unfamiliar, to note a disagreement with the author, to express agreement with the author, to highlight a sentence that is especially well phrased, or to mark a passage that is not clearly understood. There are lots of reasons for marking a text, but each reader should be able to explain what his or her annotations are there for.

In class on the day you begin discussion of this chapter, you can ask several students to tell what they marked in the Forster essay and explain why. Discuss how the markings helped to understand the meaning of the text. The idea is to be sure everyone is clear about the reasons for marking and to discover if their markings are, indeed, meaningful.

16

PRACTICING MARKING IN CLASS

Since marking an essay like Forster's is somewhat subjective, you next want to ask your students to mark a section of our instruction, which is the kind of writing that exhibits as little ambiguity as possible. Tell them that they are reading strictly for information (not much interpretation needed or desired), and ask them to identify the main point of each paragraph and, if possible, to underline the main idea (the thesis) of the section. The brief section entitled "Refocusing" on page 8 will serve nicely. But if you think that selection is not challenging enough, you could choose an essay from the Anthology of Informative Writing and pick out a suitable paragraph or two. Keep the reading short, though, as you need to allow time for careful reading and marking in class before you discuss the results.

Now, this time when you go over with the class how various people marked each paragraph, you can be a bit more prescriptive about what constitutes a good identification of the main point and what misses the point. Research done by reading specialist Karl Taylor bears out the fact that unskilled readers often cannot identify the main idea in an expository paragraph. You need to find out whether any of your students are unable to distinguish major ideas from minor supporting points. If some of them cannot tell the difference, they need the kind of active reading practice that we recommend in this chapter. The ability to identify main points in a piece of writing is important to succeeding in college classes because it underlies the ability to understand ideas and summarize material.

Postreading (p. 14)

We deliberately chose a fairly challenging essay to illustrate active reading so that students can see the need to think about what they've read after they finish and to draw inferences for a complete understanding. They will probably be able to see also from class discussion how much can be gained from talking about the reading.

BUILDING INFERENCE SKILLS (p. 16)

What we commonly call "reading between the lines" may introduce a skill that is unfamiliar to many in your class. Ask whether they have questions about this section. If later in the semester you discover that some students are not grasping the full meaning from their reading, you might want to return to this section and review Harvey Weiner's valuable suggestions for drawing inferences.

Keeping a Journal About Your Reading (p. 17)

You may want to require your students to keep a reading journal during this course in which they keep a record of everything they read--their personal responses to the reading and perhaps a brief summary of its contents. You can also have students do their prereading assignments in their journals. By requiring them to keep a journal, you stress the importance of reading and, at the same time, provide extra practice in writing.

It will be necessary, of course, for you to collect these journals every other week or so to be sure that all students are doing the assignments. But you need not correct these journals; they are intended for the students' benefit--writing as a mode of learning. All you need to do is write an occasional comment and give a grade of "check," "check plus," or "check minus." Most instructors consider the time spent in evaluating journals worth the effort. They can be a valuable source of information about what's going on in the class and how well your instruction is succeeding.

SUMMARIZING AND OUTLINING AFTER READING (pp. 17-19)

As a take-home assignment, ask your students to outline and then summarize the selection they marked today in class. At the beginning of the next class session, ask several to put their outlines on the chalkboard for the class to examine and discuss.

You will want to glance at their summaries to discover how much more time to spend in teaching them how to outline and summarize material. You need not grade the papers, of course. A "check," "check plus," or "check minus" will do.

Make the Commitment (p. 20)

If time permits, have a class discussion about scheduling time to read actively and respond to the readings. Each student needs to discover how long it takes him or her to read a page when actively engaged with the text. Once the students know their individual reading rates, they can schedule their study time with some accuracy for each assignment. Focus on realistic goal-setting.

Writing for Others (p. 20)

Be sure your class understands the difference between the kind of writing done in a journal for their own benefit and writing done for an audience--for other people who may want to read their writing. Have students list the audiences for the writing they have done in the last week: for example, 1. Self (grocery list); 2. Roommate (note about locking the outer door); 3. Best friend (letter home); 4. Professor (history homework); 5. Self (class notes); 6. Landlord (complaint about bikes in hall).

PURPOSE IN WRITING (pp. 20-21)

Ask the students to give further examples of writing that is meant to express, to entertain, to inform, and to persuade. You may be able to use today's campus newspaper to find these examples. And stress once more the fact that in reality the purposes are often mixed since aims frequently overlap.

PREWRITING ACTIVITIES (p. 21)

You may want to shorten this assignment by asking your students to choose just one purpose and write a single response. The papers should also be brief--about a page. Ask for volunteers to read aloud samples of each purpose.

Who Are My Readers? (p. 22)

This brief introduction to the idea of audience can be augmented through class discussion. For example, you might ask your students to analyze the audience they would target if they were writing letters to the editor of their local city newspaper. What would they avoid in writing to such an audience? What common feelings and beliefs would they want to appeal to? Then, change the audience to the readers of their campus newspaper and ask them how their approach might be different.

Look back at the *Writing for Others* list. Ask students to tell how the intended readers of their writings affected the way they wrote. For example, the notes and letter to the roommate and best friend might include in-group slang, the items written for oneself might use a private shorthand, and the complaint to the landlord was probably in full sentences and attempted standard spelling and punctuation.

PREWRITING ACTIVITIES (pp. 22-23)

These assignments focus on audience. You will probably again ask your students to choose one out of the three. Or you can save time and paperwork by having the students complete these assignments in groups of three or four. Assign items to groups to make sure they're all covered, and have the final products read aloud. Do not ask for polished drafts yet. Read the papers to make sure that they show some understanding of Forster's essay and especially that they reflect in their diction and level of usage some attempt to address the chosen audience.

Vocabulary Building

One valuable fringe benefit of reading is the resulting increase in vocabulary. Reading widely is, in fact, the best way to increase vocabulary because the words are learned in a meaningful context. We encourage you to give vocabulary tests--either announced or as pop quizzes--to insure that students do put some effort into learning new words.

We believe that every student should own a desk-sized dictionary and be instructed at the beginning of the semester in how to use it. Make sure that your students understand that the brief definitions found in paperback pocket-sized dictionaries are too concise to be useful and are often incomplete as well. These dictionaries can be used for spelling, but that's about all they are good for.

The quizzes you devise to keep your students on task can include any or all of the following types of vocabulary exercises.

1. Provide a list of words and ask students to use each one in a sentence of his or her own devising.

2. Provide a series of sentences with blanks where the vocabulary words belong. Then, list the words in a jumbled order, perhaps including one too many. Ask students to fill in the blanks correctly from the list.

3. Provide partial sentences, each containing a difficult word, and ask your students to finish the sentences in their own words. Example: Because of her *illicit* behavior, _____.

4. Provide five or six difficult words, and ask students to use all of them in a paragraph. Try to make sure that the words have some connection so that the paragraphs will make sense.

Chapter Two

WRITING FROM READING (p. 25)

This chapter takes the student from close reading to the first draft of an essay. Many of the topics that are covered briefly here are far more expanded in future chapters. However, since we like to get the students started writing essays early in the course, this overview helps give them some quick guidance. The chapter refers to the essay "My Wood" from Chapter 1 and includes a new essay, "The Art of Keeping Mum." It also sketches out the process of writing a draft of an essay on unemployment. Therefore, you have several examples from which to work. Following are classroom discussion questions and activities keyed to each section of the chapter.

The Prewriting Process (p. 26)

Use these questions to begin the consideration of this important first stage in the writing process:

How many of you stew and worry about a writing project before you get started?

How long do you tend to put it off? Till the day before it's due? The night before?

What goes through your mind while you are stewing and worrying?"

Generating Ideas (p. 26)

Begin by asking, "How do you usually get an idea when you have some freedom about your paper topic?" Ask students to describe how they went about choosing a topic and coming up with ideas for a recent paper in another class.

DIRECTED QUESTIONING (p. 26)

Bring a common object to class, like an Oreo cookie. Go through the six questions with the cookie as "the topic." Have the students give possible answers to each question. (We actually pass out Oreos to everyone to help inspire them.) Be sure to point out when the answers could lead to essay topics.

FREEWRITING (p. 27)

Practice a five-minute freewriting in class, using "My Wood" as a jumping off point.

21

BRAINSTORMING (p. 27)

Choose a campus problem or issue and have students brainstorm for solutions or points of view.

PREWRITING ACTIVITY (p. 28)

After students are through with their freewritings, you might have them exchange papers and underline ideas that could be developed into paper topics on each other's freewritings.

What Point Should I Make? (p. 28)

"What is a definition for the word *thesis*?"

"What other thesis ideas could come from the idea of things that have negative effects on human character?"

Help the students make a list of other conditions that bring out the worst in us.

The Drafting Process: "The Art of Keeping Mum" (p. 30)

This sample essay will appeal to students, many of whom have lived in reconstituted families. All students will at least know someone in a reconstituted family.

"Brad Goldfarb talks about getting a perspective on what his two mothers gave him. He feels that this perspective is part of becoming an adult. What else do you have to get perspective on as part of becoming an adult?" Essay topics may develop from this discussion and be used in class discussion of the next few sections.

How Do I Write about Essays? (p. 34)

"Let's list on the board the five ways the book suggests to get started on an essay idea based on a reading."

How Should I Organize My Ideas? (p. 35)

"Did you ever get part-way through a piece of writing and suddenly come up with a much better topic or plan?" Share your own experiences with having inspirations while writing.

GETTING STARTED (p. 36)

"Jot down a working title for one of the essay ideas you have developed through your prewriting activities."

STRUCTURING YOUR ESSAY (p. 36)

"Why can't you just write down your ideas in the order they come to you? After all, they all relate to the same thesis."

MAKING A PLAN (p. 36)

Ask students about their feelings about outlines. Some will have learned such a rigid system that the outline becomes a trap. Some are so hung up on the format of an outline that they lose sight of its purpose. Others have never used one. Someone--perhaps you--will bring up the practice of making an outline *after* writing the paper when the assignment requires an outline. Most of us have done this. Point out that now it's considered a good way of checking the structure of your finished essay. Try outlining Goldfarb's essay.

ARRANGING YOUR IDEAS (p. 37)

Review the definitions of logical and chronological order. "Why might you choose chronological over logical order? Why might you choose logical over chronological?" Help students see that chronological is best only when time is a critical element in the essay, such as when giving instructions in order, telling a story that leads to a climax, or showing how a problem develops over time.

Developing Your Ideas (p. 39)

Have students look at one of their own essay ideas and jot down the answer to "What do I need to know to understand this idea?" Students can discuss in small groups plans for developing ideas. "Is the paragraph from the Halvorsen essay (pp. 39-40) in logical or chronological order? Why?"

How Should I Begin? (p. 40)

Assign students to bring in opening paragraphs from magazine articles that made them want to keep reading. Read these aloud and discuss why they are appealing.

Postpone If Nothing Comes (p. 41)

This is invaluable advice, and many of your students have never heard it. Point out that your writing is likely to be at its stiffest when you first start, and the introduction will come more easily after you're warmed up.

WRITE AN APPEALING OPENING (p. 40)

"Can you visualize the scene at the unemployment office? What else do you see there?" Emphasize the idea of putting a picture in the reader's mind--a visual image.

STATE THE THESIS (p. 41)

Look again at the opening sections of the magazine articles students brought to class. Because magazine essays usually have much shorter paragraphs than expository essays, note that the thesis idea may appear shortly after the opening paragraph in magazine writing. Consider the bluntness or indirection of the various thesis ideas.

How Should I End? (p. 42)

Read the Forster and Goldfarb endings out loud while students just listen. Note that these endings have a sense of conclusiveness or closure to them: you don't expect the essay to go on.

POSTPONE OR WRITE AHEAD (p. 42)

Emphasize that no part of the essay has to be written at exactly the time you come to it. Give your own examples of times when your closing has come to you while still writing the body of the essay. We have even written the closing *first* when so moved.

WRITE AN EMPHATIC LAST SENTENCE (p. 42)

Explain further the echo or frame technique, in which the closing refers back subtly or directly to the opening.

Composing the First Draft (p. 43)

"How do you usually write the first draft of your essay? What are the good points of your method? What do you wish were different about your method? Do you try to get every spelling, every piece of punctuation, just right on the first draft?" Stress the fact that each writer must find the best personal way to work; however, also point out that most practiced writers leave a lot of decisions and corrections hanging until they are done with the whole first draft.

Chapter 3

THE REWRITING PROCESS (p. 45)

In this chapter, we provide students with an overview of the rewriting process in order to make it clear that revision involves more than changing a word here and there and correcting the typos. We think student writers should understand that major alterations will occur in this stage, that careful revision is crucial to effective writing. So, we include here advice for helping students discover what needs to be changed and techniques to help in the rewriting. We offer two separate checklists--one for revising and one for proofreading--to reinforce the need to do both. Then, to let students observe revision in action, we reproduce the first draft of a student paper responding to E. M. Forster's "My Wood," followed by a protocol the student wrote explaining why she made the changes she did in her revision and by the revised paper itself.

Discussing all of this important material, even briefly, makes for a long chapter. You may want to break it into three portions, especially if you intend to assign the revising activities and go over them in class. You could cover improving organization and coherence in one period (through p. 53), take up sentence-level revisions on the second day (through the top of p. 57), and deal with diction and the sample revision (to the end of the chapter) during the third period. It might be possible to cover sentence-level and word-level revisions in a single class, if you want to wrap up this chapter in two days and move on to the reading and writing assignment in the next chapter. You can treat much of this chapter as a preview of strategies and concerns that will be expanded and put to use throughout the course of the semester.

What Is Revision? (p. 45)

Becoming a good self-editor is the first step toward becoming a good writer. Developing writers need to discover what to do to improve their drafts. Your comments will help them, but peer revising (often called peer editing) provides hands-on practice. By reading each other's work critically and getting feedback from interested classmates, students begin to see their writing in a different way. They're not just writing for the teacher anymore; they develop a clearer, more realistic sense of audience.

Another effective way to demonstrate revision is to model the revising process

25

for the students. You can compose your own draft of one of the assignments or use a paper from another class. Write a passage on the board or on a transparency, leaving lots of space between lines. Ask the class for suggestions, and make the changes they suggest. Let them watch you scratch out words, replacing them with better choices. Let them see you move a sentence from the end of the paragraph to the beginning or delete an example that's off the topic or add a detail to clarify a point. They will see that writers do not turn out perfect prose on the first try; they will see how writers explore and experiment in order to find the best way to express their thoughts.

Revising from the Top Down (p. 46)

If you decide to model the revising process, you can also demonstrate the logic of following a top-down approach to revision. Be sure to take up matters of content and structure first, and show how they affect the other elements of writing. Suggest to the students that it doesn't make sense to focus too soon on such features as phrasing or punctuation or word choice, since they may end up being cut or significantly recast. Once the larger issues are settled, then turn the attention to details of mechanics and style.

What Should I Add or Take Out? (p. 47)

Not all writers work from a detailed outline, but making an outline of a draft, as we suggest on p. 47, is an efficient way of checking organization and development. As an instructor, you can examine an outline in a matter of minutes in a conference or during class, if you're running a workshop in which students do much of their writing under your supervision. You can quickly point out where a writer has strayed from the thesis or where there are gaps in thought or where a point needs to be moved. (Chapter 8, by the way, will provide further advice about ways to organize material.)

CHECKING OUT A PARAGRAPH (p. 48)
You can have students work in groups on this activity. Ask each group to come up with an outline and put it on the board for comparison with the others. Use the questions following the paragraph in the text to practice inventing specific details for expansion and support. (Chapter 9 explains various techniques for developing ideas.)

What Should I Rearrange? (p. 49)

If you want to analyze arrangement strategies further, have students examine the structure of Maya Angelou's "Graduation" (p. 124), which uses logical organization in the first five paragraphs and then follows a chronological arrangement in the rest of the selection. Many of the paragraphs in Brad Goldfarb's essay "The Art of Keeping Mum" (in Chapter 2) are arranged logically: they start with a general idea and add specific details and explanations to support that idea.

Does It Flow? (p. 50)

Use paragraphs from the essay in Chapter 2 ("The Art of Keeping Mum") to illustrate the concepts in this section. Students will be familiar with the content and will be able to focus on the presentation. The first paragraph (p. 31) shows how a writer follows up on readers' expectations. Because it opens with a statement about a photograph of "two mothers," readers expect to hear more about that photo and those mothers. Goldfarb meets that expectation by describing the photo as a way to identify and give some details about his mother and his stepmother.

Paragraph 4 (p. 31) of Goldfarb's essay illustrates "downshifting." You might want to rewrite it on the board with indentations (as we did with the paragraph on p. 52) to show how the points shift down from general to specific. Ask students to find other paragraphs that exemplify downshifting. Also ask them to look for transitional expressions in the Goldfarb essay. You can follow this analysis by putting students in groups or pairs to work on the REVISING ACTIVITY (p. 53), which provides practice in improving paragraph coherence. As time permits, ask the groups or pairs to share their revisions with the whole class.

What Sentences Should I Combine? (p. 53)

Sentence combining is useful for eliminating unnecessary repetition, for focusing the readers' attention on main ideas, and for creating a pleasing variety of syntactic structures.

SENTENCE COMBINING ACTIVITY (p. 54)
    The sentences in this exercise can, of course, be effectively combined in a number of ways. Here's the way we would do them:
1. Forster explores the changes in mental attitude brought about by his purchase of a piece of land.

27

2. He uses four arguments to prove his contention that ownership has caused him to seek power and control.
3. Forster feels an irrational desire to enlarge his holdings by doing away with his neighbors.
4. That his property is constantly being invaded and littered prompts him to consider ways to fence out human intruders.
5. Forster's typically British sense of humor is quiet, understated, and subtle.

REARRANGING FOR EMPHASIS AND VARIETY (p. 55)

Explain that most of the sentences we write are not emphatic. We mostly write periodic sentences in which we reel ideas out of our heads, adding phrases and clauses until we decide to put in a period. But good writers must be able to compose a rousing, emphatic sentence when the need arises--for concluding sentences or introductory sentences or for sentences that convey key ideas. Nobody is born with this skill. We learn it by noting effective sentences that others have written and by consciously or unconsciously imitating such sentences--in short, through observation and practice.

WRITING ACTIVITY (p. 56)

We would increase emphasis and conciseness by rewriting the sentences this way:
1. A happy man Mark Twain was not.
2. After promising to become a Christian and go to church faithfully, he married Olivia Langdon.
3. Although he failed to become a Christian, he did go to church faithfully--at first.
4. His good friend Joe Twichell ministered to the affluent congregation of what Twain called "The Church of the Holy Speculators."
5. Even though Twain upheld the highest morals and ethics, he could not accept the Old Testament God--a God who struck him as too vengeful, too jealous, and too cruel.

What Words Should I Change? (p. 57)

Most of use rely heavily on those "weatherbeaten" verbs in the list on p. 57, especially in the early stages of composing when precise, vigorous wording is not a primary concern. It's during revision that we can take time to put a little zip into our words. The exercise is designed to make students conscious of the need to improve word choice and sentence structure when revising.

28

REVISING ACTIVITY (p. 58)

Students may revise the sentences in a number of interesting ways. Here are our versions:

1. As a child, I considered my parents omniscient.
2. I was certain they wielded control over all our lives.
3. My mom exuded confidence; Dad fed the livestock, plowed the fields, planted the corn, harvested the crops.
4. Now, being married and struggling to raise a family myself, I realize that Mom and Dad were not as secure as we kids thought.
5. Surely they suffered moments of doubt as they sought to stretch their slim resources to feed and clothe six hungry, growing kids.

USING ACTIVE AND PASSIVE VOICE (pp. 58-59)

Students are often taught to use the formal third person when they write. All too often they end up composing stilted sentences that rely on passive verbs (to avoid the first person). We believe that students should use passive voice when it is appropriate, but they also need to realize the strength and economy of writing in active voice.

REVISING ACTIVITY (p. 59)

We would rewrite the exercise sentences this way:

1. I think Forster used the raspberries to illustrate how ownership creates greed.
2. Forster first described them as "not plentiful."
3. Then they became a prized possession that other people could gather easily.
4. People could also pull up the foxgloves.
5. Forster appropriated these naturally growing plants as his rightful possessions.

CHOOSE YOUR WORDS CAREFULLY/ATTEND TO TONE/CHOOSE AN APPROPRIATE LANGUAGE LEVEL (pp. 59-61)

These sections on diction are intended to make students more aware of the value of precise word choice. During the revising stage, careful writers examine their language carefully to make sure that the both connotations and denotations are precise and accurate. Tone and usage level are matters that everyone should consider before beginning to write, but the revising stage provides a chance to make adjustments and check for consistency. Don't worry at this point if the students are a little vague about some of these considerations; they will have opportunities to enhance their knowledge in subsequent chapters.

Observing Revision (pp. 61-69)

Ask students to compare the two versions of the paper. To ensure that they understand the changes that Ami made in her revision, assign students (singly or in pairs or in small groups) to match up recommended changes with the revised version and report their findings to the class. Ask one student (or pair), for example, to note all the marginal comments in the first paragraph and to check if the advice was followed and where the specific changes occur in the revision. You might also read the protocol aloud and ask students to locate the changes. For instance, Ami says she moved her own thoughts to the beginning of every paragraph: ask students if they can how and where this revision was made. You can also ask students these questions: "Do you think the revisions were effective? Was anything changed that you think should not have been? Do you have suggestions for other revisions that would improve the paper further?"

Revision Priorities (p. 69)

Encourage students to revise with a plan in mind and to revise in stages. Here is a useful revision agenda that composition expert Maxine Hairston recommends (*Successful Writing*, 3rd ed., pp. 93-94):

> 1st: Plan to do as little revising as possible when writing the initial draft.
> 2nd: Consider the priority of the assignment; if it has a high priority, allow time for several drafts.
> 3rd: Make major changes first. Concentrate on the substance; wait until later to do the fine tuning.

This approach may seem like a lot of work, but it can save time and energy in the long run. And many writers find that it works.

PART TWO

EXPRESSIVE WRITING (p. 73)

Since in our experience expressive writing comes most easily to students, we begin with this aim. It offers students a chance to focus on themselves as communicators, to develop a sense of self as writer which will underlie the other modes, in which the audience visibly dominates. As your students write the assignments in this section, keep an eye out for subjects that they may develop into informative or persuasive pieces later.

Chapter 4

READING EXPRESSIVE WRITING CRITICALLY (p. 75)

Unfortunately, we find that our students aren't likely to have had any instruction in how to go about reading material that is not already inherently interesting to them or that seems difficult to them. Having no tools to work with, they are prone to give up the job in defeat. In this chapter we attempt to give them some tools. The material here reiterates the advice in Chapter 1, on the whole.

From the outset, emphasize that reading is not a passive activity. You might discuss in class the ways that students presently read assignments. Ask what setting they find the most productive for reading assignments and why. Discuss how *set* or frame of mind also influences reading comprehension. Try to come up with some guidelines about the proper set and setting for reading assignments.

Choose from the class discussion and activity suggestions we give below according to your students' needs and the time available. At this early stage in the semester, you probably don't want to dwell too much on details and fine points of interpretation. Many of the strategies and techniques that are introduced in these opening chapters will be practiced and reinforced in subsequent chapters.

Identifying Characteristics (p. 76)

"What are the four questions to ask as you try to identify distinctive features of an essay?" We relate these four questions to "My Wood"; in class, you might apply them to "The Art of Keeping Mum" from Chapter 2.

Sample for Critical Reading (p. 77)

The overview is one of the most important steps in critical reading. Have your students read the biography of Lam in class; then ask, "What kind of person is Andrew Lam?" Through this discussion, students will have background that will prove valuable as they read "My Vietnam, My America."

ANALYZING THE OVERVIEW (p. 82)

Begin by asking: "What imagery in the opening paragraph suggests strong feeling?" We overview the Lam opening for the students. You may want to bring in opening paragraphs of other kinds of writing (humor, fiction, how-to, technical, and so on) and discuss the expectations that these openings set up. As alternatives, you could use openings of other essays chosen from within this text or ask the students to bring in openings to discuss.

MARKING THE ESSAY (p. 82)

Go over the list of activities suggested by Adler and Van Doren. You might even ask your students to memorize the list in order to be sure that they take it seriously. Study the annotated essay, at least in part, together in class. As you go through the essay again, ask students what markings they would add. Mark the essay yourself ahead of time, and share some of your comments and queries with the class.

Checking Your Understanding (p. 87)

Emphasize the usefulness of writing responses out so they do not remain vague. Holes in comprehension will be more obvious when students try to express understanding in writing.

"Can you think of other ways that our country's war experiences in Vietnam are blended into our present society?"

Dealing with Confusion (p. 87)

Encourage students not to give up when they find material difficult. If possible, give an example of reading that *you* must struggle with (computer manuals? rhetorical theory? economics?). Finding an understandable chunk, relating it to other chunks, and visualizing are useful approaches.

In or outside of class, have students apply critical reading techniques to another short essay. Some good choices in this book are Dick Gregory's "Shame" (in Chapter 5, p. 95), "Darkness at Noon" by Harold Krents (p. 172), and "A Hanging" by George Orwell (p. 175).

Chapter 5

ILLUSTRATING A POINT: NARRATIVE (p. 91)

This chapter is aimed at helping students learn to write brief narratives to use as illustrations in other types of expository and persuasive essays. Writing about personal experiences is not just a form of self-expression; it is, besides that, a method of demonstrating and explaining, of inducing readers to feel and think and believe the way the writer does. Students need to be reminded that narratives also can be useful in producing effective introductions.

What Is Narrative? (p. 91)

Most students will associate narrative with telling stories, and that is certainly one way to define this mode of discourse. But narrating occurs in all kinds of speaking and writing situations, from everyday conversations to official reports and scientific treatises. The major source of narrative material is memory--memory of our own experiences or of accounts told or written by others. To demonstrate this point, ask your students to write down what they were doing yesterday at this exact same time of day. Have them write down their recollections and read them aloud to one another in small groups (or to the whole class). The chances are that these accounts will be dominated by narrative writing.

You can also define narrative in a more literary sense by talking about *plot* and *chronology*. Movies and TV shows are great sources of plots to examine in discussion. At this point, it is probably not necessary to get technical or detailed: a general grasp of what a plot is and how it is used to organize events will be sufficient.

READING MORE NARRATIVES

Before you ask your students to write their own narrative essays, you may want to assign several more from the Anthology of Expressive Writing in this text to increase their understanding of what makes a narrative effective. Some suitable choices:

Maya Angelou, "Graduation" (p. 124)
Dave Barry, "Getting Your Goat" (p. 136)
Marcia Ann Gillespie, "Delusions of Safety: A Personal Story" (p. 151)
Harold Krents, "Darkness at Noon" (p. 172)
Elizabeth Wong, "The Struggle to Be an All-American Girl" (p. 220)

34

In this Instructor's Manual you will find for each of these selections a number of discussion questions as well as additional ideas for writing. Your students may find these topics more appealing than the ones included within this chapter. The more choices you provide for them, the more the likelihood of their finding something that strikes a chord and will produce good writing.

Prewriting: Analyzing Effective Stories (p. 98)

The prewriting questions following the narratives by Hughes and Gregory are intended to help students see how narration functions as a writing strategy for presenting ideas in a dramatic, convincing way. Students should be encouraged to write out their answers in full because writing will make their thoughts visible and allow them to see when their thinking gets fuzzy or off the track. They can examine what they have written and revise or expand their responses. Here are some reasonable answers.

1.   Hughes's piece is concerned with disillusionment and the loss of naive faith. His "salvation" from the conformity of enforced belief is accompanied by his disappointment and sadness because the religion did not turn out to be what he was told it would be--and hence was not the satisfying, comforting faith that he so wanted it to be.

Gregory's account touches on several important issues: the effects of poverty and racism on the human spirit, the need for validation and acceptance as a person, as well as the cruelty and inadequacy of charity and welfare.

Thesis for Hughes: Ironically, when I was "saved" at age thirteen, I lost my childish faith.

Thesis for Gregory: Poverty and racism are cruel in their destruction of the essential human need for self-respect.

2.   Both accounts involve betrayal by adult authority figures. Both also tell about painful lessons that force the central character to grow up fast and leave some childhood belief behind. The adults in both selections are insensitive, incapable of understanding the children they are in charge of, unaware of the effects that their power and grown-up attitudes are having.

Thesis for both essays: Children cannot be forced to believe or behave the way adults want them to.

3.   The young Hughes finally gets up because he realizes that he has been deceived--the religious experience will not turn out the way he has been told it would. His tears are ironic because they are not tears of joy (at having found religion, as his aunt thinks) but tears of disappointment (at having lost

35

his faith). The title is similarly ironic: Hughes was saved *from* religion, not *by* religion. He says that it was "the last time in my life but one" that he cried to stress the importance of this event and how profoundly it shaped his emotional and spiritual being.

4. Gregory means that we all have some dream or hope that must be relinquished, some goal that cannot be attained, some loss that we never really recover from. Helene Tucker's face haunts him because it represents failure and shame to him; it is the one image that, more than any other, reminds him of his poverty and his oppression. Helene Tucker meant so much to him: she had become a symbol of all that he wanted but could not have because he was poor and black in a society that values being rich and white.

5. Dialogue is dramatic and engaging. It authenticates the incidents by making them seem real. Readers are put into the middle of a scene, where they can listen themselves to what was said. But direct quotations lose their power if overused. They are also not useful for conveying background information. Summarizing is more efficient and allows the writer to keep a balance between important ideas and lesser ones.

Writing (p. 100)

Narrating involves selection and arrangement of details and events. Either before writing or after completing a first draft, a successful writer gives conscious attention to both processes. Doing a large measure of this thinking before writing is probably more efficient than simply diving into a narrative and trying to straighten it out, or flesh it out, or thin it out later. But different people have different writing processes. You should allow your students to follow the process that works best for them.

Still, we encourage students to think and plan before writing. During this prewriting stage, they can explore their topics in depth, generating as much material as possible before they attempt to shape it into a continuous narrative. Many students will find that they need to stimulate their memories through freewriting, list-making, or just talking about relevant past experiences with classmates or friends. These activities will provide the raw material from which the narrative can be drawn.

Also, a period of incubation will give their unconscious minds a chance to probe the memory banks further. Thus, it might be helpful to leave some time between first making the writing assignment and requesting a first draft. If time permits, allow students to work on invention during class, especially at the beginning of the semester while they are exploring the techniques.

36

Rewriting (p. 101)

Our advice in the text focuses on improving dialogue and creating scenes. Both of these devices are fairly sophisticated, and you may want to model some of the skills involved. Ask for a volunteer (or choose one beforehand, using the paper anonymously). If your students did not produce any suitable scenes, take one from Orwell's essay "A Hanging." Put whatever scene you choose on the overhead projector, and show the class--perhaps on the board--how you would rewrite the passage in order to reduce that scene to a summary. Then, work with the class to rewrite it once more to turn the summary back into an effective scene.

REVISING ACTIVITY (p. 102)

This exercise may seem rather mechanical but should serve to make students examine their narratives closely. You might point out that they may need to experiment with these revisions. They may rewrite a passage and like it less well after they finish. Such an effort is not wasted, though, as even accomplished writers try out revisions that they later reject. It's all just part of the process of perfecting one's prose.

COMBINING SENTENCES (p. 103)

If you have time as you are reading the first drafts, mark two places where a couple of sentences could be effectively combined. Look for unnecessarily repeated words as well as for short, choppy sentences. Then ask the students to combine each sentence in two different ways.

Put your class in groups; ask them to look at each other's sentences and decide which of the two revisions they like better--and, if possible, explain why.

REVISING ACTIVITY (p. 105)

After your students have tried their hands at recasting Maya Angelou's ideas into effective sentences, you may tell them to look at her essay "Graduation" (p. 124, ¶ 2), and see how closely their versions resemble hers--and decide which they like better.

Chapter 6

DEVELOPING A WRITTEN VOICE (p. 107)

A writer develops "voice" from the available resources of language: words, sentence patterns, punctuation, paragraphing. While most students usually have only a general concept of what voice might be, they often find it an interesting subject to study, not only because it offers something new and different for them to work on but because it also involves an element of fun in changing words, shifting sentence parts, and playing with words. In this chapter we ask students to read and listen to someone else's voice--in order to learn how to develop and refine their own.

Listening to Voice: "Under the Influence" (p. 108)

Since voice is related to the impression that a writer makes on his or her readers, you can ask students to think about what kind of person Sanders is. Here are some questions they might consider during and after their reading:

How does Sanders present himself to you?
To what degree are you aware of his presence in the writing?
Does he seem distant and detached, or is he 'up close and personal'?
How do you think he wants you to feel about him?
Is your impression of him important to his purpose?

Prewriting: Comparing Voices (p. 117)

The material in this section directs the student's attention to the way that voice establishes a connection between writer and reader and, therefore, how voice relates to audience and purpose. It's important for developing writers to become more conscious of just how much their purpose and their intended audience affect the way they write.

WRITING ACTIVITY (p. 118)
The exercise in looking for vivid modifiers, strong verbs, figurative language, and rhythmic sentence patterns is one that you do right along with your students. You can point out one of each to get things started.

Before you begin, you may want to define and illustrate figurative language. You can explain that figurative language involves deliberate deviation from the

38

ordinary (literal) meaning of words. Ask students to explain why the following sentences cannot be interpreted literally:

> This assignment is a piece of cake.
> Their relationship is on the rocks.
> His backhand is a little rusty.
> I'm running out of steam.
> Our teacher is falling apart.
> Things are finally looking up for me in this class.

Then ask them to restate the sentences in ordinary, non-figurative language: "This assignment is easy." You can also ask them to explain the implied comparisons in these statements, which all use metaphors, and to consider what emotional qualities are suggested. For example, the sentence about the relationship implies a comparison with a boat that has hit the rocks along the shore and is disintegrating or "breaking up." Such a comparison, which suggests a disaster, doesn't hold out much hope for reconciliation. A more neutral literal version ("They're having problems with their relationship") doesn't have the same impact.

OTHER VOICES (p. 118)

These contrasting passages show how voice changes according to purpose and audience. It's not necessary to analyze each passage fully, but you might want to make sure that the students understand and agree about the way the alternative voices are described ("transparent or neutral," and "stern, confident, yet reassuring"). If you want, read the two passages aloud and ask students to describe how they feel about the author. "Which presentation do you prefer?"

Writing (p. 120)

It is important that students choose to write about something that they know and care about. Familiarity and some emotional involvement makes it easier to develop a distinctive, appropriate voice. Also emphasize the value of having a strong sense of audience and a clear purpose in mind for each of the three parts of the assignment.

Tell students that they can begin with any of the three short essays (they don't have to start with #1). Point out that the pieces are interrelated (in subject matter) and that working on one will help with writing the others.

Rewriting: Balancing Sentences (p. 121)

As you read the first drafts, put an X in the margin beside sentences that you think can be varied or improved.   Limit your suggestions to a reasonable number: changing more than one sentence often involves changing others. If you use peer review, direct the student readers to make suggestions for variation in the same way (by placing an X or some other mark in the margin). Sometimes you can use a few examples from student papers to demonstrate what the whole class should be trying to do.

REVISING ACTIVITY (p. 122)

Parallelism and balanced sentences are stylistic concepts that may need to be illustrated further, if you have time. Having students imitate model sentences is an effective instructional technique. On the board or overhead projector, write several sentences (perhaps some of the "rhythmic" sentences that the class found in Sanders's essay), and mark each into structural units--to help students see what they should imitate.   Point out patterns (phrases, clauses, series) and structure words (conjunctions, prepositions, subordinators, determiners). Then show how you would imitate these models. Finally, give the students five or six sentences to work on (individually or in groups). Unlike many drills and exercises, sentence imitation has been shown to carry over into the students' own writing. For this reason, you may want to repeat this stylistic practice from time to time during the semester. You can find sentences to imitate in the essays in the anthologies.

ANTHOLOGY OF EXPRESSIVE WRITING

In the three anthologies included in this text, you will find essays to use as additional readings to supplement the instruction in the preceding chapters. Composition experts acknowledge that in large measure becoming a competent writer involves becoming a competent reader. So, have your students read as widely as possible in these anthologies.

In this Instructor's Manual we provide apparatus to enable you to use these selections in class, if time permits. We include here a brief discussion of each essay identifying the major ideas and pointing out useful rhetorical techniques. We also offer ideas for prereading journal writing, recommendations for constructive comparisons between essays, and further suggestions for discussion and writing.

GRADUATION (p. 124)

MAYA ANGELOU

The thesis of Angelou's essay is a condemnation of the oppressive racism which destroys the happy mood of her long anticipated graduation and which will circumscribe the lives of the graduating class as well as the entire black community. Angelou makes the readers feel the injustice of racial prejudice by first presenting a compelling picture of her naivete and innocence, her confidence that through hard work and intelligence she can be whoever she wants to be. She provides plenty of evidence to show how important education is to this rural black family (Bailey's gift, the store's closing, her mother's solicitude), and these details make the child's disillusionment even more poignant.

In the expertly dramatized scene depicting the graduation ceremony, Angelou introduces the cold reality of racism through the attitudes of the insensitive white bigot who delivers the commencement address. But with the singing of a Negro anthem and the delivery of Henry Reed's valedictory speech, the narrator regains her hope and confidence. The essay closes with a ringing endorsement of black pride: "I was a proud member of the wonderful, beautiful Negro race" (¶ 61).

41

Before the class reads this essay, you might have your students recall their own graduation day and record in their journals what their own emotions, hopes, and dreams were at that time.

Comparative Study

Have your students read Elizabeth Wong's "The Struggle to Be an All-American Girl" (p. 220). Discuss the similarities of these youthful narrators undergoing a crisis of identity because of belonging to an ethnic minority. What notable differences are there in these two essays, particularly in the endings?

Ideas for Discussion and Writing

1. Why do you think yellow was the color chosen for the dresses of the little girls in the graduating class? What associations do you have with this golden hue?
2. Why does Angelou include all the details of the preparation for the graduation ceremony? How do these passages contrast with what follows?
3. Why does she include the scene in which brother Bailey presents his gift? What does the gift reveal about the character of the narrator?
4. Contrast the black minister's message to the graduates (¶ 17) with that of the white politician (¶s 37-39).
5. When it turns out that there are not enough chairs on the stage after the two white men arrive, who has to leave (¶ 33)? Why does Angelou include this detail?
6. Angelou never states her theme, but we get her message powerfully and clearly. What is it? Why does she leave her thesis unstated?
7. Can you assess the importance of the narrative voice in contributing to the success of this piece? In other words, why is the child-narrator an effective rhetorical strategy for conveying this theme?
8. Have you ever directly experienced racial prejudice or bigotry of some kind? If so, construct a narrative in which you reveal what happened to you. If possible, dramatize a scene or two. Do not state your thesis; let it come through in what you write, as Angelou's message does.

GETTING YOUR GOAT (p. 136)

DAVE BARRY

Barry's humorous piece is a good example of contemporary satire, a writing genre that pokes fun at human behavior, sometimes gently, sometimes scathingly. The tone here seems fairly gentle, although that doesn't mean Barry's not serious about his complaints. And what are they? Primarily the essay satirizes the commercialism of Christmas and all the accompanying marketing techniques, like "The Little Drummer Boy" piped through the Muzak system in every department store and the commercials that urge kids to demand expensive toys. The story about "the Christmas goat" may or may not be making fun of the numerous manger scenes that spring up during the holiday season.

The humor stems from several sources. One device is Barry's adoption of the persona of "Uncle Dave," reminding us that holidays are traditionally the time for families to get together. But in Barry's version folks celebrate with "too many eggnogs" instead of more appropriate reflection on the Savior's birth. Although he never states his thesis, we get the point through the mention of "the Index of People Living in Refrigerator Cartons" and "the true meaning of the holiday season, which is to stimulate the economy" (¶ 2). We are allowed to conclude for ourselves that "the true meaning of the holiday season" would be expressed by helping those homeless people instead of throwing money away at the "Toys Sure 'R' Costly" store (¶ 8).

Prereading Journal Idea

Ask your students to think about Christmas--to remember certain songs or traditions that they associate with this time of year. Have them record these details and conclude by expressing how they feel about the holiday season.

Comparative Study

Read Eudora Welty's "The Little Store" (p. 206). Consider the contrast between the child's pleasant excitement at going to the grocery store for her mother and Barry's jaded complaints at having to go to the department store to buy his wife's gift. What has changed to make these shopping ventures so different?

1. Can you describe the tone of this essay--that is, the author's attitude toward the events he is describing?
2. What do you call the rhetorical device that Barry uses when he refers to himself throughout the essay as "Uncle Dave"?
3. Why does Barry refer to George Bush as "*Uncle* President Bush" in paragraph 2?
4. Why do you think Barry mentions in paragraph 2 that "the economy seems a tad sluggish, as measured by the Index of People Living in Refrigerator Cartons (IPLRC)"?
5. What is the point of this piece? Is it stated or merely implied?
6. Why do department stores play Christmas music endlessly from Thanksgiving until Christmas? Does it annoy you?
7. Barry's essay is contemporary satire--that is, poking fun at some foolish or annoying social practice or human behavior. Think of some traditional event or typical behavior that bothers you the way the hokum associated with Christmas bothers Barry. Then write a satire. You might consider fraternity initiations, senior proms, fancy weddings, bungee jumping, smoking cigarettes, family reunions, or the like.

PICKING PLUMS: FATHERS AND SONS AND THEIR LOVERS (p. 139)

BERNARD COOPER

Although this narrative is basically chronological, we do get flashbacks. These excursions in the mind of the author into the past are important because they allow Cooper to establish his father's character through dramatized scenes--the two most memorable being the flinging of the suitcases and the recounting of his mother's death. We also get information about the past through the present-time narrative--for instance, when the father tells about falling out of the plum tree.

The narrative remains focused on Cooper's father and his somewhat stormy relationship with Cooper's mother until paragraph 18. Here Cooper introduces a new connection between father and son: each has a secret kept from the other. Then the author reveals that his father is having an affair with a woman and that he himself is having an affair with a man. By accident, Cooper meets his father's lover--a much younger woman who is also of a different race. While caring for his father after the fall from the plum tree, the author reveals that he is gay; his father seems to take the news well. In the final paragraph we get unifying echoes of earlier elements--the plum tree and the flying suitcases. The author's final observation, though, leaves the situation uncertain--like life: "I wondered whether nothing or everything would change."

Theme is not easy to identify since this is largely a character sketch of the father, but an important part of the essay concerns the difficulty that gay people face in coming out to their parents.

Prereading Journal Idea

Think about your relationship with your father. How do you get along with him? Narrate an episode you shared with your father that seems to capture his personality and the way you feel towards him.

Comparative Study

Read Susan Allen Toth's "The Boyfriend" (p. 190), which describes a relationship the author maintained throughout high school with her "boyfriend." Compare this piece with Cooper's memoir depicting his relationship with his father. Which essay allows us to enter more deeply into the lives being presented? Why?

Ideas for Discussion and Writing

1. How would you describe Bernard Cooper's father when he was a younger man? How has he changed by the time his son is writing about him?
2. Why do you think Cooper entitled this piece "Picking Plums"? What associations can you make with plums?
3. What technique does Cooper use at the beginning and the end to unify his essay?
4. Cooper implies that his father's profession in some subtle way influenced his father's personality. Explain how. Do you think this interpretation is a rationalization, just making an excuse for his father's behavior--or do you consider the explanation valid?
5. What rhetorical purpose does paragraph 18 serve?
6. Father and son each has a secret lover. What is there about the two lovers that makes both relationships to some degree socially unacceptable?
7. Cooper dramatizes several scenes in his memoir, often reproducing conversations. Why do you think he does this? Why did he choose the scenes that he did?
8. Have you ever had a good friend or family member reveal to you that he or she

45

is gay? If so, write an essay describing this experience, how you felt, and how this knowledge affected your relationship with this person. Try to dramatize the scene in which you found out.

ON RECEIVING THE NOBEL PRIZE (p. 149)

WILLIAM FAULKNER

Faulkner's Nobel Prize speech is a fine example of elevated formal rhetoric in the expressive mode. His message of hope is one that young people still need to hear. Although we no longer stand in dread of nuclear destruction, other social ills have sapped the ability of the younger generation to look forward to better times: drugs, crime, a languishing economy, lack of jobs and career opportunities. We need hope as desperately today as we did when Faulkner delivered his call for young writers to bolster the human spirit.

Of the many effective rhetorical techniques illustrated in Faulkner's speech, one of the easiest for students to pick up is *polysyndeton*--the use of *and* instead of commas in a series to gain emphasis:

--love *and* honor *and* pity *and* pride *and* compassion *and* sacrifice. (¶ 3)

He also provides a powerful example of *antithesis* that is well worth having your students model:

I believe that man will not merely endure: he will prevail. (¶ 4)

The speech includes several admirably balanced sentences suitable for modelling, like this one:

He writes not of love, but of lust, of defeats in which nobody loses anything of value, of victories without hope and worst of all without pity or compassion. (¶ 3)

Prereading Journal Idea

Ask your students to respond to this question: Do you think that you will enjoy a better quality of life than your parents have? Explain why or why not.

46

Comparative Study

Read Martin Luther King's "I Have a Dream" speech (p. 511). What rhetorical qualities does it share with Faulkner's speech?

Ideas for Discussion and Writing

1. At the time Faulkner wrote his speech, the threat of nuclear war pervaded the minds of Americans. Is there any similar fear that now troubles the American public?
2. What solution does Faulkner propose as a means of counteracting the prevailing pessimism of his time? Would it work for us today?
3. Find an example of an extremely short sentence, and explain how it gains emphasis in its context.
4. What is the usage level of the language in this speech? Would this kind of writing be appropriate, for instance, in business writing? Why or why not?
5. Find a sentence that you consider particularly impressive and copy it exactly. Them rewrite the sentence five times supplying your own content and words each time.

DELUSIONS OF SAFETY: A PERSONAL STORY (p. 151)

MARCIA ANN GILLESPIE

Gillespie addresses a problem that troubles many people today--male violence against women. She achieves immediacy and verisimilitude by writing from her personal experience, beginning with her naivete as a young girl and concluding with her resentment at having to live in "a group under siege" (¶ 19). She shows us that many women, in order to avoid living in a constant state of fear, convince themselves that male assault can only happen to other people. Then she shows that such denial is perilous: "I was in college when I learned that it didn't just happen in certain places, to certain people" (¶ 5).

She explains how she learned caution, and in paragraph 12 she discusses the constant need for all women to use caution, running through a list of the various categories of women in our society to help us grasp the universality of the problem. She wants us to see that *all* women are at risk. That seemingly obvious statement can prove a real eye-opener for females who still believe what they have been taught since childhood--to seek the love, approval, and protection of men.

47

Prereading Journal Idea

Respond briefly to this question: Is there any place that you would feel unsafe at night on your college campus? Compare responses from females and males in class before discussing Gillespie's essay.

Comparative Study

Read Caryl Rivers's "Rock Lyrics and Violence Against Women" (p. 522) and Merrill Melnick's "Male Athletes and Sexual Assault" (in Chapter 13). These articles present possible causes for the kind of violence that Gillespie warns about. Discuss whether these theories make sense.

Ideas for Discussion and Writing

1. Why does Gillespie begin and end her essay with the mention of strawberry ice cream?
2. Why was she able to finish her ice cream as a child but now finds herself unable to eat strawberry ice cream?
3. Do you think the woman in the first dramatized incident (¶ 2) was justified in stabbing the man?
4. Gillespie says in paragraph 4: "It didn't happen to nice girls from God-fearing homes, wasn't done by our brothers, boyfriends, and fathers. No! No! No!" Why does she make that statement so emphatic?
5. What is Gillespie's purpose in paragraph 12?
6. What do you call the transition the author uses at the end of paragraph 14? Does it work well?
7. In paragraph 19 Gillespie provides an analogy to help us grasp her point. What is the analogy? Does it aid in your understanding of what she is saying?
8. If you have ever observed a woman being battered by a man, write an account of the abuse and try to analyze why the woman tolerated the violence.

WIND (p. 157)

WILLIAM LEAST HEAT-MOON

This selection illustrates informative as well as expressive writing. The author

48

provides information about tornadoes, including vivid descriptions, scientific data, and interesting folklore. We are then introduced to Paul and Leola Evans whose story constitutes the narrative, expressive portion. In order to gain immediacy, the author allows Leola to tell about the big wind in her own words.

Because she is an expert narrator, we are caught up at once by her tale. She includes intriguing details--like coming to bed in her "good rabbit-fur coat and wedding rings" carrying a "handful of wooden matches," and about the old hog, "so terrified she got between us and wouldn't leave all the way up to the neighbors'." Leola's down-home diction is also part of the appeal: "hunkered in the corner," "clamped on to each other like ticks" (¶ 7). The precise details included in her description of the tornado's aftermath (¶ 7) enable us to envision the destruction clearly.

Prereading Journal Idea

Write a paragraph or two explaining how you feel about the wind, and explain why. Do you like wind? Hate it? Fear it? Or never give the wind a thought?

Comparative Study

Barry Lopez also deals with nature in "A Wolf in the Heart" (p. 325). Do you see any similarity in the way each writer approaches his subject? Can you describe the tone that they share?

Ideas for Discussion and Writing

1.   Why would the preacher think that "Giving names to nature is un-Christian" (¶ 1)? Can you tell what the author's attitude is?
2.   What typical weather pattern causes tornadoes in Kansas?
3.   Why does the author let Leola tell the story of the tornado in her own words?
4.   What do you think makes Leola a good storyteller?
5.   What makes the final sentence an appropriate closing? Consider how, for instance, it relates to the beginning of the selection.
6.   Have you ever seen or been involved in a catastrophe of some sort--a flood, a fire, an auto accident, a plane crash, a hurricane, or a tornado? Describe the event with specific details chosen to convey to your readers your feelings at the time of the disaster.

DOWN AND OUT IN CHICAGO (p. 161)

EUGENE IZZI

Izzi's first person account conveys with great conviction how it feels to be a homeless person in a large city like Chicago. In his first dramatized incident he also makes us understand the danger and helps us see how little a human life matters to those who prowl the streets at night looking for helpless prey.

Izzi's account is not intended to present solutions to the horrific problems caused by inner city poverty. He just wants us to see things as they really are. We are given details that perhaps we never thought about before: the lack of a toilet, of a shower, of a toothbrush, of fingernail scissors, of fresh clothes, of a place to come in out of the rain. Perhaps his major purpose is to let us see how poverty and homelessness degrade the human spirit. When he must stand on the street and beg for change, he is a diminished man. We see his rage when he is hungry and has money but is refused service in a convenience store because of his filthy, bedraggled appearance. And we see him do nothing to retaliate, revealing to us the powerlessness of the poor and homeless.

Prereading Journal Idea

Imagine yourself homeless in Chicago (or some other big city)--quite literally living on the streets. List in order of importance the things you would miss the most.

Comparative Study

George Orwell's "A Hanging" (p. 175) is quite different in subject and setting, but like Izzi, Orwell is trying to elicit sympathy for someone who is being treated like an inanimate thing--not a human being--and is powerless to help himself. Compare the attitudes of Orwell's executioners with the attitudes of the people Izzi encounters on the streets. How do both authors emphasize the humanity of the unfortunate people they are writing about?

Ideas for Writing and Discussion

1. Why does Izzi refuse to go to a shelter while he is pretending to be homeless in Chicago?
2. What is your response to the dramatized incident in which he is attacked during his first night on the streets?

50

3.   What sort of mental change does Izzi experience when he becomes a person begging for spare change? What is the attitude of most of the people he encounters?

4.   What has been your attitude when approached by a person begging? Do you think your feelings may change as a result of reading Izzi's account of being homeless?

5.   How does Izzi change physically during his time as a homeless person?

6.   Why does he include the story about the businessman who gives him five dollars and then fails to recognize him later when he tries to return double the amount of money?

7.   What do you think Izzi's major purpose is in writing this article?

8.   Write a first-person account detailing an occasion when you found yourself in an environment where you felt isolated or perhaps even threatened. Try to make your account as dramatic as Izzi's by using conversation and plenty of well-chosen specific details.

PHOTOGRAPHS OF MY PARENTS (p. 168)

MAXINE HONG KINGSTON

In this excerpt from one of her best-selling books, Kingston uses an interesting device to characterize her immigrant parents--old photographs. But since we get only the sketchiest impression of her parents, we can detect an additional purpose: to present a glimpse of the culture from which they came. The snapshots of her father emphasize the difference between the light-hearted, fun-loving Americans and the serious-minded, dutiful Chinese.

What we know about the mother we learn from her pictures and from the Chinese diplomas attesting to her medical degree (¶ 1). We are told her age and a bit about how she looks, and "she is not thinking about her appearance" (¶ 3). In the other picture she is "not soft" and "not humorous" (¶ 4). The narrator concludes, "She is intelligent, alert, pretty. I can't tell if she's happy" (¶ 4). We know that the father is happy; even while at work in the laundry he is smiling. The father's carefree existence contrasts sharply with the mother's somber life. And the differences between two people are reflected in the distinctions between two cultures.

Prereading Journal Idea

Are your parents similar in their personalities--both cheerful perhaps or both unhappy? Both talkative or both quiet? Or are they quite different? Write a brief character sketch of your parents, emphasizing how they are alike or different.

Comparative Study

Most of the time the first-person approach is used to achieve believability and immediacy--the feeling that you are right there almost observing events as they are described. How is Kingston's use of the first person different from other first-person essays in this book? Do you still find it effective? How else could she have presented her material?

Ideas for Writing and Discussion

1. , What do we learn about Kingston's mother from the old photographs?
2. What do we learn about her from the scrolls?
3. What do we learn about the father from the snapshots? Why did he go to America? Where does he live? What sort of job does he have? What does he do in his leisure time? What sort of person is he?
4. Why is it that "Chinese people do not smile for photographs" (¶ 3)?
5. In this essay, what do we see as the major contrast between the ancient Chinese culture and the newer American one?
6. How is that contrast conveyed in the essay?
7. Is our culture still frivolous and fun-loving? If not, write an essay detailing our national characteristics.

DARKNESS AT NOON (p. 172)

HAROLD KRENTS

Krents manages in this short essay to voice a protest about his treatment as a blind person, yet he makes his point with such wit and charm that we never feel we are being reprimanded. He uses sarcasm but in a humorous way. His dramatizations of the difficulty he encounters in restaurants (¶ 4) and of the incident in the hospital with the translating orderly (¶s 5 - 14) make the embarrassing scenes comical--especially the last line in which the orderly repeats to the elderly lady, "He says he doesn't need an interpreter," showing that both parties are insensitive.

Krents organizes his essay according to his three complaints: people think "since my eyes don't work, my ears don't either" (¶ 2); "others know that of course I can hear, but believe that I can't talk" (¶ 4); and "the toughest misconception . . . that because I can't see I can't work" (¶ 15). He concludes with an amusing story about the neighbor child who couldn't tell who was blind, Krents or his father, because both shot baskets so wildly. This brief narrative perfectly illustrates the point he wants to make: that physically challenged persons should be treated just like everybody else.

Prereading Journal Idea

Ask students to respond to the following question: Which of your senses is most important to you?. Explain why.

Comparative Study

In "Getting Your Goat" (p. 136), Dave Barry also adopts a humorous tone in order to convey a serious complaint. Besides the tone, what other elements in these two essays are similar?

Ideas for Writing and Discussion

1. What important piece of information does Krents convey in his introduction?
2. What are his three complaints about the way he is treated as a physically challenged person?
3. What is the tone of this essay?
4. What does the tone contribute to the effectiveness of the piece?
5. Does it seem egotistical of Krents to mention his academic honors at Harvard and his Oxford degree? Why does he include these details?
6. Krents never states his thesis, but what point is he making?
7. Currently we are encouraged not to call people either *disabled* or *handicapped*, two words that Krents used in 1976 to describe himself. Today we are supposed to use the terms *differently abled* or *physically challenged* instead. What do you think about such language? Can you think of other similar terms that are currently in vogue? Write an essay in which you either explain why these expressions are socially useful or complain that they rob the language of force and meaning.

A HANGING (p. 175)

GEORGE ORWELL

Orwell's essay is a masterful protest against capital punishment. Not only are we shown how a human being is destroyed by the execution, but we also see how the men conducting the hanging have their humanity diminished by their distressing task.

The descriptive detail is, in a word, perfect: "a sodden morning," "a sickly light, like yellow tinfoil," cells "like small animal cages," "a puny wisp of a man" with "vague liquid eyes," guards "like men handling a fish," and so on.

The introduction of the dog is a stroke of genius, as it gambols about "wagging its whole body, wild with glee," the very personification of life amidst the march to death. Like the condemned prisoner, the dog is "half pariah." Dogs are expected to growl and snarl instinctively at bad people, but this one dashes up to lick the prisoner's face. After the prisoner is hanged, the dog whines and retreats from the frightful scene.

In paragraph nine the narrator observes the prisoner suddenly stepping "slightly aside to avoid a puddle in the path." This human action surprises the narrator then into speculating on "the unspeakable wrongness of cutting a life short when it is in full tide," the only time the narrative shifts from the dramatization of the event into the mind of the narrator.

We realize that the superintendent, who appears so gruff and callous, is probably an agreeable chap who simply has an unpleasant duty to perform and wants it over with as quickly as possible. We see his basic decency when he allows the condemned man's prayer to go on and on, even though, as the narrator confesses, "the same thought was in all our minds: oh, kill him quickly, get it over, stop that abominable noise!" When the prisoner is finally dead, the unbearable tension is released, and "All at once everyone began chattering gaily." The men indulge in what is quite literally gallows humor, but the narrator observes in the final chillingly ironic line, "The dead man was a hundred yards away."

Prereading Journal Idea

Did you ever go along in a group with an action you knew to be quite wrong? Describe what happened and how you felt during and after the event.

Comparative Study

Richard Selzer's "A Question of Mercy" (p. 180) also deals with death, but in the Selzer piece death is desired because a young man is suffering from AIDS. Compare the moral and ethical issues raised in these two works.

1. What descriptive words and details set the mood in paragraph 1? What is that mood?
2. Why are we never told the prisoner's name or the crime he committed?
3. Why is the appearance of the dog in paragraph 5 described as "a terrible thing"? What purpose does the dog serve in heightening the pathos of this scene?
4. Why does the superintendent appear so irritable before the hanging? Why are all the officials in such a good humor following the prisoner's death?
5. What paragraph gives the main point of the essay? How does the puddle episode relate to it?
6. Does the change of mood after the hanging support or detract from the main point? Explain how.
7. Can you explain what makes the final line so effective?
8. Rewrite this grim drama from the point of view of the prisoner, describing the thoughts and feelings running through his mind.

A QUESTION OF MERCY (p. 180)

RICHARD SELZER

Selzer's unrelenting honesty in recounting this narrative is perhaps what contributes most to its power. By dramatizing his involvement with the dying young man, Selzer allows those of us who have been untouched by the tragedy of AIDS to see the suffering and debilitation wreaked by the disease. The descriptions are almost too grim to read, and yet we do read them with both pity and aversion because the tale is threaded with suspense and moral ambiguity.

Selzer plunges us at once into his dilemma: should he break the law and end the anguish of the suffering man? As a medical doctor he is sworn to preserve life. But the dying man's friend reminds him that sometimes laws can be wrong: sometimes mercy lies in ending the agony. Here Selzer briefly recounts a couple of events from the past (narratives within a narrative) that illustrate the need to provide mercy (¶s 9-13), as if to convince himself, but probably more to sway his readers.

Once Selzer has visited the dying man and seen for himself the grim details (¶s 27, 32, and 36), he makes his decision: "And I am convinced." Probably he refrained from giving us all of those details in consecutive paragraphs lest they overwhelm us. We are given particulars of the young man's life in Columbia which make him a real person, not just a "case," and we also are told some facts about his lover. Although the men are referred to only by their first initials to protect their privacy, Selzer wants us to see them as blameless, loving human beings.

A good portion of the narrative is devoted to the plans for providing an easeful death. But, despite the careful arrangements, the sufferer does not die and must be removed to a hospital. Now the victim indicates that he does not want to die, that he wants treatment, but he cannot speak because of the tube thrust down his throat. We assume that his nod is intended to let Selzer off the hook. So he dies fifteen days after the attempt at euthanasia. What would have been so wrong about ending his life a mere fifteen days earlier? We may speculate, but Selzer does not. He retains his objective dramatization to the end, allowing us to draw our own moral conclusions.

Prereading Journal Idea

If someone you love dearly were suffering a certain and agonizing death and begged to die and be released from misery, would you try to engage a doctor (perhaps someone like the Michigan doctor with the "suicide machine") to assist your loved one in committing suicide? Discuss why or why not.

Comparative Study

See the suggestions above for comparison of Selzer's essay with Orwell's "A Hanging" (p. 175). Or compare this essay's ideas about death with those in "Death in the Open" (p. 531) by Lewis Thomas.

Ideas for Discussion and Writing

1. Do you consider Selzer's introduction effective? Explain your response.
2. Why would this essay be less effective if the author had written it without conversation?
3. What is the purpose of the narrative in paragraphs 10 through 12?
4. Where in the essay does Selzer make his only direct statement in favor of euthanasia?
5 Why do you think Selzer provides us with details of the dying man's earlier life in Columbia, about his being gay, and his problem with most of his family's lack of acceptance?
6. What do you think of Selzer's phrase in paragraph 21, "the abominable gymnastics of writing"? Can you explain what he means? Why would a

famous and expert writer feel that way about writing?

7. Do you consider Dr. Selzer a "coward" (¶ 94) for reneging on his promise to be present at the planned death? Explain your response.

8. Another famous physician-writer, Dr. Lewis Thomas, feels that we have "tangled and evasive attitudes about death" in this country. Write an essay discussing how Americans deal with death.

THE BOYFRIEND (p. 190)

SUSAN ALLEN TOTH

Toth's memoir of her adolescent courting may be nostalgia for the older generation, but for some young people today it may seem like fiction. She writes about pre-Madonna days in which virginity was not something to be ashamed of, when "nice girls" did not "do it." But many of the tensions and embarrassments associated with dating and sexual attraction that she describes are still common today.

Toth adopts a plain, breathless style that mimics the thought processes of a teenager and allows readers to remember the psychology of their own early dating trials. We are reminded of the importance of the automobile in these rituals. But in Toth's day the activities were apparently limited to the front seat. Her ability to laugh at herself--evidenced most clearly in the episode in which she responds to her first kiss by returning a lick on the cheek--contributes to the charm of the essay. It has no apparent theme, but its purpose is to recreate for modern readers the muddled comedy of adolescent love as it was played out in the 1950s and to present a nostalgic look back for those readers who were there.

Prereading Journal Idea

Ask your students to record the most embarrassing incident they ever experienced on a date. You may want to caution them to observe the bounds of good taste in case you ask anyone to read his or her account aloud to the class.

Comparative Study

Toth's essay is written in the first person but differs from most of the first-person accounts in this anthology because she does not dramatize the events, as for instance Selzer and Orwell did in their essays. Why do you think she chose the approach that

57

she did? Would the piece be more effective, do you think, if the events were dramatized?

Ideas for Discussion and Writing

1. How does Toth engage the reader's interest in her introduction?
2. In paragraph 2 Toth talks about "necking." What does that mean? Do we have a current slang term to describe the same, rather limited activities?
3. Describe the differences you can observe between what dating was like in Toth's time and today?
4. What embarrassing mistake does Toth admit to making right after her first kiss?
5. What do the last two sentences of the essay tell us about the way young women have been enculturated to feel about males?
6. Probably this essay doesn't have a theme, but can you state its purpose?
7. Take the embarrassing episode that you wrote about in your prereading assignment and rewrite it from the point of view of the other person on the date.
8. Consider the difference in attitudes toward sexual attraction and male-female relationships presented in this essay and Marcia Ann Gillespie's "Delusions of Safety" (p. 151). Have the relations between the sexes changed that much in thirty years? Or was the violence simply a well-kept secret in Toth's era? Write an essay referring to both pieces in which you discuss these issues.

A LIGHTNING PILOT (p. 197) and A CUB PILOT'S EXPERIENCE (p. 200)

Mark Twain

Twain's classic essays reveal for us the lost art of riverboat piloting without benefit of radar and other sophisticated devices in use today. The river still shifts, but instruments now tell the Captain where it has gone. Twain's anecdote about the "lightning pilot" is an example of his storytelling at its best. In the first paragraph he gives us all the information we need in order to understand how hazardous an undertaking it was to take a steamboat through a blind crossing at night. We also get the crucial knowledge that Mr. X, the expert pilot, is a sleepwalker, a "somnambulist." After this careful preparation, Twain turns the narration over to Ealer, the pilot on duty, and allows us to observe the tension as Mr. X takes over the wheel in these perilous waters. The humor lies in the unexpected twist at the end of the tale when Ealer discovers that Mr. X performed his masterful piloting while sound asleep. Only Twain could have written the closing line, in which Ealer marvels,

58

"And if he can do such gold-leaf, kidglove, diamond-breastpin piloting when he is sound asleep, what *couldn't* he do if he was dead!"

The second selection recounts Twain's actual experience as an apprentice riverboat pilot. He wrote this piece long after he had left that profession when the river was closed down by the Civil War. He never returned to piloting, but his pen name is taken from riverboat jargon. In those days the depth of the water beneath the boat was measured by a man using a long pole, who called out the depth of the water. "Mark twain" means two fathoms--safe water--the call that every pilot wanted to hear.

So there is some nostalgia involved in the account, but the primary purpose is to relate the astonishing difficulty of learning to "read" the river. For this purpose Twain adopts his favorite persona, presenting himself as a "conceited ass," to use his own phrase. Most of the humor stems from the naivete of this persona as he calmly ignores all the information being presented to him by the infinitely patient Mr. Bixby. We are well prepared when that gentleman finally explodes and unloads "a volley of red-hot profanity." The nostalgia is most apparent at the end in the description of the sumptuous appointments of the "big New Orleans" steamboat. Again Twain closes with a perfect line, quite in character for his persona--and perhaps for Twain himself: "And when I found that the regiment of natty servants respectfully 'sir'd' me, my satisfaction was complete."

Prereading Journal Idea

Do you know a good "shaggy dog" story? A shaggy dog story is a long story with lots and lots of details, seemingly unnecessary details, that finally concludes with a silly punch line. Write your story, taking great care to make it as funny as possible.

Comparative Study

Compare the technique employed by Twain in "A Lightning Pilot" and William Least Heat-Moon in "Wind" whereby they turn their essays over to a character in the narrative and allow that person to dramatize the story. Why is this rhetorical strategy more effective than if each author had continued telling the story in his own voice?

Ideas for Discussion and Writing

1. Why does Twain give us all that information in the first long paragraph?
2. Why does he shift the narrative voice and allow Mr. Ealer to finish telling the tale?
3. Can you analyze what makes the punch line funny?

4. Twain's "gold-leaf, kidglove, diamond-breastpin piloting" is a kind of metaphor. What non-metaphorical adjectives might you substitute for his? What is lost?
5. Describe the persona adopted by Twain in "A Cub-Pilot's Experience." Why is it effective?
6. The last paragraph shifts from the account of the cub-pilot's learning the river to a description of the "big New Orleans boat." Why do you think Twain included this last paragraph? Does it make a fitting conclusion?
7. What is Twain's purpose in this piece?
8. Pretend that you are writing your own autobiography. Choose an incident in which you learned something the hard way and describe the experience. You may want to adopt a persona as Twain does--present yourself as a naive, pompous person who lacks good sense.

THE LITTLE STORE (p. 206)

EUDORA WELTY

Welty takes us back to an era about midway between Twain's pre-Civil War description of steamboating on the Mississippi and Toth's account of dating rituals during the 1950s. Welty says that she is writing about the time of the World War I Armistice, so we can assume that the visit to the little store must have taken place in 1918.

She begins with details of the halcyon life she enjoyed as a child in her comfortable middle-class household. We are told about the imaginative toy she created and the games she used to play, but suddenly we are given a puzzling sentence following her description of the little store: "Above the door a little railed porch ran across on an upstairs level and four windows with shades were looking out. *But I didn't catch on to those*" (¶ 9, italics added).

The narration proceeds just as if she had not dropped this hint of something mysterious about the dwelling upstairs above the Little Store. She goes right on with details about the merchandise to be admired by a small child, the difficulty of deciding how to spend the nickel received in change, and the excitement of going home "the hard way" through the storm sewer. Not until paragraph 22 does she end the suspense by returning to the "story" that was taking place at the Little Store, "one that was going on while I was there," but which she completely overlooked.

And we never find out what happened--only that "There was some act of violence" (¶ 23). The children in the Welty family are never told--and if Welty found out later when she was older, she's not telling us. Her point lies not in the nature of the violence but in the mystery of its being there all along and yet totally unperceived

60

by her. Without knowing it, she was, even as a child, "on the track of" the "facts of life, or death" (¶ 25). She concludes by introducing the problem of illusion versus reality that permeates all our lives.

Prereading Journal Idea

Describe a favorite place you liked to visit as a child. Try to convey how it made you feel to be there.

Comparative Study

Welty lets us see that in her childhood she was sheltered from unpleasant experiences--especially from violence. Marcia Ann Gillespie in "Delusions of Safety" (p. 151) shows herself as a child of about the same age observing a bloody, violent action. Discuss how society has changed in the intervening seven decades with respect to children and their exposure to violence.

Ideas for Discussion and Writing

1. What kind of atmosphere does Welty create in the first few paragraphs of her story?
2. In what paragraph does she first introduce an element of suspense?
3. In what paragraph does she return once more to the mystery she hinted at earlier?
4. What do we learn about the young Eudora Welty as she describes her trip to and from the Little Store? What kind of child was she? What details reveal traits of her character?
4. What was the mystery of the Little Store?
5. Why did Welty's parents not tell the children what happened?
6. Why does Welty not reveal to us exactly what occurred?
7. How does the mystery relate to the theme of the essay which is obliquely revealed in the final paragraph?
8. Write an account of some mystery you encountered as a child, something concerning sex or violence perhaps. Include at the end of your essay how you felt when you were finally old enough to discover the truth.

THE GEESE (p. 213)

E. B. WHITE

This essay provides an example of what is called the plain style, in which the writer appears simply to be conversing with the reader in everyday language. In reality that simple language is crafted as carefully as a sonnet. The main charm of White's piece lies in his affectionate presentation of the geese as "companions" (¶ 2). They are testy and capricious rather than friendly, but White clearly values them for their personalities, for their seemingly human quirks and failings. To the author these creatures are not simply farm animals. The old gander is a "widower," with "nobody to swap gossip with" (¶ 4), and is "full of sorrows and suspicions" (¶ 7) after losing his mate of many years; later we are told that "ganders take an enormous interest in family affairs" (¶ 15). White seems just to be describing his geese as he sees them.

We learn a good deal about geese, but the purpose of the essay is not informative. But the chief interest is to show the rivalry between the two male geese build to a climax: "It was an awesome sight, these two great males locked in combat, slugging it out--not for the favors of a female but for the dubious privilege of assuming the responsibilities of parenthood" (¶ 16).

In order to make sure we do not miss his point, White draws the comparison between goose and human behavior even more sharply: "I felt very deeply [the old gander's] sorrow and his defeat" (¶ 17). Then we are shown the younger generation who will succeed the old, the goslings "climbing in and out of the shallow pan for their first swim . . . " (¶ 18). And finally, the author must dispose of the unhatched eggs, "the unlucky ones," and he concludes, mourning his own mortality: "I don't know anything sadder than a summer's day" (¶ 19).

Prereading Journal Idea

Describe in your journal the personality of a memorable pet, giving the pet human qualities and showing how you related to each other.

Comparative Study

Study the style--that is, the word choice, the sentence length, the sentence structure, the level of usage, the figures of speech, the sound of the prose--of Mark Twain's "A Lightning Pilot" (p. 197), Orwell's "A Hanging" (p. 175), and White's "The Geese." What elements do they share in common? Discuss which of the three essays you like best, and explain why.

1.   What is there in the introduction that sounds an echo in the conclusion and subtly prepares us to perceive the theme?
2.   Why does White give his geese human characteristics, as when he describes the old gander as a "widower" with "nobody to swap gossip with" (¶ 4)?
3.   "Winter," observes White, "is a time of waiting, for man and goose" (¶ 10). What associations do you have with winter, especially as you consider the changing of the seasons in the endless cycle of nature?
4.   What are the two male geese battling over near the end of the essay?
5.   Why does the author identify with the old gander rather than with the triumphant young male?
6.   Why does White conclude with the observation that "I don't know anything sadder than a summer's day"?
7.   How does that final ironic line help to convey the theme of the essay?
8.   There is a truism that young people are unable to envision the possibility of their own deaths. If you think this observation might be true, write an essay discussing several kinds of typically rash adolescent behavior that seem to validate a feeling of immortality among young adults.

THE STRUGGLE TO BE AN ALL-AMERICAN GIRL (p. 220)

ELIZABETH WONG

Wong wrote this essay when she was only twenty-one years old, but her skill as a writer is apparent in every paragraph. The details are perfectly chosen to illustrate her childish distaste for the older, more stoical Chinese culture. The essay conveys a clear message about the power of conformity on children. Wong shows us through her personal testimonial how determined children are to be just like everybody else. Even if we are native to the culture, we recognize the universality of the behavior she reports. We find her conclusion poignant and persuasive, as she says, "At last, I was one of you; I wasn't one of them." Then, in an abrupt reversal, she reveals her change of heart: "Sadly, I still am."

Prereading Journal Idea

Record some incident during your childhood when you were made to feel like an outsider. Maybe your clothes were wrong, your accent different, your haircut unstylish, your legs too fat, your color not the same as the majority of the children. How did you react?

Comparative Study

Eudora Welty in "The Little Store" (p. 206) adopts the persona of her child-self, just as Elizabeth Wong does. Discuss how the same rhetorical strategy can produce such different effects when the author's purposes are dissimilar.

Ideas for Writing and Discussion

1. How does Wong's introduction draw you into the essay?
2. Why does she adopt the persona of herself as a ten-year old child?
3. In what city did the narrator grow up? If you had not read the headnote, could you have guessed from reading the essay?
4. Why are she and her brother so determined in their rejection of the Chinese culture?
5. What effect does Wong achieve by ending paragraph 8 with a single word punctuated as a sentence?
6. What third culture is introduced in paragraph 13, in which Wong declares herself "multicultural"?
7. What is the effect of the final line of the essay?
8. Have you ever found yourself in a culture that is "foreign" to you? It might have been a cultural difference stemming from class background, ethnic customs, sexual preference, or religious beliefs. Write about the differences you saw and felt between your culture and the foreign one. If you have not yourself had such an experience, interview someone who has--perhaps an exchange student--with the aim of writing about the cultural differences.
9. Did you ever do something to conform? Describe what happened and how you feel about the experience now.

PART THREE

Chapter 7

REPORTING INFORMATION (p. 225)

Informative writing rests on a clear, direct transaction between writer and reader. Writers use information for many reasons: to instruct, to give directions, to present facts, to define, to explain ideas, and to support opinions. In all of these exchanges, writers want their readers to accept the information, which means that the writers must establish their authority and demonstrate the correctness of their data. In short, informative writing must be convincing.

Looking at Informative Writing (p. 226)

Carol Ezzell's essay on the mating problems of tree frogs is both entertaining and informative. Her humorous, informal approach, however, does not take away from the accuracy and scientific validity of the information she is conveying. The researchers may not know what to make of their findings, but the details of their study--both its procedures and its results--are intriguing. This is scientific writing that should appeal to all but the most technically impaired of readers.

Analyzing Informative Writing (p. 229)

The answers to the 10 questions are given in the text. You can review this material to see if the students have any questions or want to add further points to our discussion of the informative strategies that Ezzell uses.

Prewriting: How Do I Report Information Effectively? (p. 231)

You might point out that writers often begin gathering information with only a general notion of what they want to write about. They sometimes have a clear purpose and

65

a definite audience in mind, but just as often they let the material shape and refine their goals. This give and take between writer and subject is a familiar component of the writing process. Inexperienced writers usually have to learn how to let uncertainty work for them and not be intimidated by it.

PRINCIPLES OF INFORMATIVE WRITING (p. 232)
The three principles of informative writing are adapted from James L. Kinneavy's discussion of the aims of writing (*Writing in the Liberal Arts Tradition*, 1985, chapter 4). Kinneavy recommends the method of indicating sources within the text, using the author's name in the attribution ("According to historian Barbara Tuchman, . . .") and giving the page number in parentheses at the end of the quoted or paraphrased material. You can find further examples of documenting sources informally in Carol Ezzell's essay, pointing out where she cites her sources by name (¶s 5 and 15) and even works in the name of a printed source (¶ 7). (Ezzell does not supply page numbers.) This approach will probably work well for papers in this section on informative writing. Full documentation is discussed in Chapter 13.
Writing is informative if it has both content and surprise value. The statement "California is a western state" is true, but it conveys no information: it has content but no surprise. Readers judge the information value of a piece of writing by how much they learn from it.

Writing: Using Primary Sources (p. 232)

A student's first impulse, when assigned an informative paper, is to run to the library and start looking for books and articles on the subject. Although this is a very good way to gather more information, it is not the only way. People are often excellent sources of information, and interviews can provide writers with substantial material to write about. It is surprising how often people can supply valuable facts and ideas. And every college campus is filled with experts on a variety of topics, many of whom are willing to talk with students about their work.
To help students prepare for their interviews, have them write out a series of questions and practice interviewing a partner. You can also model the procedure by arranging to interview a guest speaker--a colleague from another department, for example, or a local artist or business person. These activities will give students a feel for the process and will also help to reduce anxiety.
The information that your students gather in their interviews is likely to be interesting and informative to the whole class. When possible, set aside time for students to read their finished drafts to their classmates; let others ask questions and make comments. The writers who share their work will gain a valuable sense of accomplishment.

WRITING IDEAS (p. 234)

If you think your students aren't familiar with feature articles (ones that use interviews), gather some examples and bring them to class. Look in the Tempo or Living sections of daily newspapers, consult the Sunday supplements (like *Parade* or *The Chicago Tribune Magazine*), or try the school newspaper (many schools have a weekly feature supplement).

Rewriting (p. 235)

If students have read their drafts in class or in groups, they can proceed through the revision section of the chapter on their own. If you want to conduct a revision activity, have the class look at the sample student essay together and discuss the ways that the student writer, Stephen Beeson, varies his use of quoted material. Also point out where Beeson summarizes, paraphrases, and adds his own comments and observations. Then assign the rewrite as directed on p. 237.

Chapter 8

ORGANIZING AN ESSAY (p. 239)

Though we avoid attempts to cram pieces of writing into patterns of development like cause and effect and comparison and contrast, we do believe that learning to identify these patterns within essays is of benefit to the beginning writer. These patterns should become part of the writer's repertoire of rhetorical choices.

The Basic Structure: Beginning, Middle, and End (p. 240)

Though this structure may seem overly obvious, you might point out that when a piece of writing just "feels" wrong, the cause might be that it doesn't fulfill the reader's expectations about each of the three basic parts.

Looking at Chronological Order: "With the Chernobyl Victims" (pp. 240-41)

For background, you might bring in or ask students to look up accounts of the 1986 nuclear power plant disaster at Chernobyl. This study will explain the essay's setting of urgency and excitement.

PREWRITING ACTIVITY (p. 251)
Other technical exposition in the Champlin essay appears in paragraphs 24-25 (how amount of exposure is determined), paragraphs 28 (explanation of fetal liver transplant), and paragraph 32 (how a bone marrow transplant is performed).
The students are free to choose a term or operation to explain. You might begin by discussing terms or operations in your own field or hobby (for example, *set induction* in teaching, *lead* in journalism). Then brainstorm a list of terms or operations that have special meanings in college life (*section*, for example, or *final* or *catalog*).

Writing: Supporting Your Main Idea (p. 251)

WRITING ACTIVITY (p. 251)
You could start the exercise by doing the first one on the board as a whole group. The others can be expanded by individual students or by groups. Have volunteers read some of the results out loud.

68

SELECTING DETAILS (p. 252)
   This is a tricky subject. When details are or are not relevant may seem very subjective.
   Ask your students, though, to think of an acquaintance or relative who seems to take forever to tell a story, whom they constantly feel like asking to get to the point. *These* are people who have no sense of selection of detail.

Writing Ideas (p. 252)

These topics offer opportunities for a lively mixture of expressive and informative writing. Encourage your students to think of their classmates as the audience. After they have written first drafts, have them exchange papers and tell their partners whether the informative material is clear and complete.

Looking at Logical Order: "The Healing Power of Confession" (p. 253)

Be sure your students understand that this essay's organization is in contrast with Champlin's chronological organization. The brief outline following the essay should help them see the difference.

   You may want to discuss the content of this essay as well as its organization in class. Ask the students whether they have ever experienced relief from writing about something. Encourage them to try daily writing as an experiment.

PREWRITING ACTIVITY (p. 266)
   Our suggestions for other essays to outline are Harold Krents, "Darkness at Noon" (p. 172); Joan Didion, "In Bed" (p. 304); and Barry Lopez, "A Wolf in the Heart" (p. 325).
   To save yourself paperwork, assign an essay from the three choices to one-third of your students to outline at home. When class reconvenes, put the students in groups to compare their outlines and come up with a best version to hand in. This way, you'll only have three outlines from each class to mark.

Writing: Maintaining a Focus (p. 266)

To insure that your students know the difference between a subject and a thesis, brainstorm a list of five subjects on the blackboard. Then, as a group, make up two possible thesis statements for each subject. Insist that a thesis must be a whole sentence.

WRITING IDEAS (p. 267)

We have tried to design ideas that force the students to use organizations other than narrative. Be sure to encourage a thoughtful mixture of patterns of development.

Rewriting (p. 268)

Ask students for a post-writing outline of their essays when you collect them. Decide in advance whether you'd like to require sentence outlines: we think they are harder to write than topic outlines, but they may reveal problems with structure more clearly.

SHARPENING THE INTRODUCTION: WRITING ACTIVITY (p. 269)

The new opening for "The Healing Power of Confession" might be more expository, more directly appealing to people's concern about their own health and telling earlier exactly what the author did to research the subject. These alterations would attempt to reach a broader readership than the readers of *Natural Health*, who are already expecting a certain type of article.

You might also discuss the article's title: we found it quite misleading. "Confession" sounds to us like admitting a crime or sin, and the article actually covers more than that. Students may suggest more accurate titles for the article.

The Champlin article, if rewritten for *Natural Health*, would need to open with a more personal approach to the audience. Perhaps the health hazard of nuclear plants and nuclear bombs would be emphasized, since that is a major interest to these readers.

SHARPENING THE CONCLUSION (p. 269)

Read the sample closings aloud for effect. Some of them are taken from essays in this text; students may want to look them up.

REVISING ACTIVITY (p. 270)

If students are tired of their own essays, let them exchange papers and write new conclusions for each other. The first and second writers can then discuss the new closing.

Chapter 9

DEVELOPING THE CONTENT (p. 271)

In this chapter we discuss various methods of elaborating ideas, taking all of our examples from a single essay, Sallie Tisdale's "We Do Abortions Here." Students will learn the most common patterns of developing paragraphs so that they will have available a variety of techniques for producing out their own nicely turned out paragraphs.

How Do I Develop Ideas?

LOOKING AT DEVELOPMENT (p. 272)

Tisdale's essay, which appeared in *Harper's* (October, 1987), is rich in detail and powerful because of its inclusion of narratives, descriptions, and conversations. It certainly deserves rereading. Students will probably become so caught up during the first reading that they need to go through it again slowly paying attention to the ways in which each idea is developed.

Ask your students to study all of our comments--clear to the end of the "Prewriting" section--before they start to read the essay again. They will then know what to look for as they go over it carefully the second time.

Techniques for Development (p. 281)

After your students read this section and then go back and study the essay, they should understand the methods of development discussed here. You should, of course, ask if they have any questions concerning this material before you take up the prewriting activity.

Prewriting (p. 286)

This assignment works well when students discuss their findings in small groups. There are no right or wrong answers since taste plays a part in determining how people respond to a piece of writing. But as you circulate from group to group, encourage students to explain *why* the paragraph they chose as the most effective works so well. Try to keep their responses focused on rhetorical techniques rather than on content.

71

Writing (p. 286)

This assignment will allow students to practice several methods of developing the same idea. These compositions should be single paragraphs, not fully developed essays. Students enjoy doing these short papers; they often fashion quite creative pieces.

SUGGESTED ADDITIONAL READINGS
   If you want your students to see more examples of good paragraph development, you may assign any the essays listed below. And if you want them to write a full-length essay involving paragraph development, you will find suitable topics in the Instructor's Manual following the discussion of these essays.

   Maxine Hong Kingston, "Photographs of My Parents" (p. 168)
   William Least-Heat Moon, "Wind" (p. 157)
   George Orwell, "A Hanging" (p. 175)
   E. B. White, "The Geese" (p. 213)

Rewriting (p. 287)

You will want to stress the advice we give students in our section entitled "Finding Points That Need Development": they must read, read, read in order to become truly proficient writers. We hope that you will assign many essays in this text--as outside reading to be summarized or simply responded to in a journal, since you won't have time to discuss everything in class. You do not need to grade journals; simply read them quickly and offer comments occasionally. Writing practice helps students even if nobody marks it.

REVISING ACTIVITY (p. 288)
   We think the only paragraphs here that do not need more details and examples are 4 and 6, which are clearly an introduction and a conclusion. Even those can, of course, be improved; some of the students may choose to revise those paragraphs also. This exercise usually generates plenty of well-developed paragraphs.

REVISING PRACTICE (p. 289)
   Ordinarily, when a final draft is returned to a student with a grade on it, that piece of writing is dead. So, if you ask your students to resurrect a paper for revising (as we suggest here), be sure to promise them that you will read it again and assign another grade. Otherwise, they will lack sufficient motivation to do a good job.

TIERHEIMS: LIFESAVING ANIMAL HOMES (p. 293)

MARILYN BURNSIDE

Burnside describes how Germany deals with stray or unwanted pets. She clearly has a persuasive point, as evidenced in the closing by the direct exhortation to organize locally. However, most of the article gives a detailed description of the principles, financing, and operation of Tierheims. The author suggests that the different ways our countries treat animals reflect differences in the societies.

Prereading Journal Idea

Discuss the problem of pet overpopulation in America. If any of the students have had to take an animal to the pound, let them describe their experience.

Comparative Study

Read Barry Lopez's "A Wolf in the Heart" (p. 325), and compare the Native American, German, and mainstream American attitudes toward killing certain animals.

Ideas for Discussion and Writing

1. Why does the author believe that the Tierheim system occurs in Germany and not in America?
2. What weaknesses does Burnside see in the American system of dealing with stray and unwanted pets?
3. How are Tierheims financed?
4. Whom do you think is the audience Burnside targeted in her essay?
5. How does Burnside refute the argument that instituting a Tierheim-style system in America is expensive?
6. Why do you think Germany has the restrictions on pet ownership described in paragraph 14?

73

7. Find out how stray and unwanted pets are dealt with in your own community. If possible, visit their shelter and talk to people in the field. Write an essay that provides information about the system, using Burnside's as a model.

DOES SOCIETY MAKE RIGHT-HANDERS? (p. 298)

STANLEY COREN

Though one might expect a persuasive essay pleading that parents and teachers leave left-handers alone, this essay uses research studies to show that left-handers are not completely changed anyway. Though children, especially before the age of eight, can be taught to use their right hands for specific activities like writing and eating, the change will not generalize to other activities that are not so closely monitored. Coren's essay is an excellent example of scientific research written for a general audience. He weaves together instances, explanations, and statistics artfully.

Prereading Journal Idea

Let the left-handers in the class talk about whether they have felt pressure to change to right-handers in any way. Have they encountered any problems with being left-handed?

Comparative Study

Read Henry Dreher's "The Healing Power of Confession" in Chapter 8 for another example of scientific research written for the general public. Point out similarities.

Ideas for Discussion and Writing

1. What behavior is most frequently changed from left- to right-handed? Why?
2. How does social pressure increase the amount of visible right-handedness? Were you surprised at the percentage of left-handers?
3. What are the "diabolical associations" mentioned in paragraph 2? Do you know of other negative associations left-handedness has? For example, look up the origins of the word *sinister*. And what is a *left-handed compliment*?
4. What methods do parents and teachers use to get children to change hands?

5.   What is the "subliminal coercion" referred to in paragraph 6? What are some examples?
6.   Can handedness be changed?
7.   Interview some left-handers for an essay about attitudes and practices that affect them today.

IN BED (p. 304)

JOAN DIDION

Didion's purpose in this essay is to clear up the common misconception that migraine headache sufferers are the victims of their own imagination. She switches between first person, to accentuate her impressions, and third person, to present scientific findings that explain hereditary predispositions to the disability. When she applies the symptoms to herself, it is in a detached and yet forceful manner. her tone is dispassionate when she refers to herself and the effect migraines have on her. Her imagery is also strong, filled with vignettes of pain and suffering. Despite personal details, Didion avoids becoming over-sentimental or maudlin. If she had, the reader would dismiss her argument based on the common judgment that overemotional migraine sufferers bring the condition on themselves.

Prereading Journal Idea

Discuss the psychological causes of illness with your class to see if the general consensus is that people can make themselves sick.

Comparative Study

Read Scott Shuger's "What I Learned in School Today" (p. 389) and compare the two essays' blending of personal experience and objective fact. Compare Didion's discussion of the connection between migraines and personality with Bill Moyers's ideas about mind-body medicine (in "Medicine's New Frontier," p. 344).

Ideas for Discussion and Writing

1.   Does anyone in class have migraines? If so, is Didion convincing to a fellow

sufferer?

2. What elements of the common definition of migraine does Didion consider wrong? What elements does she consider right or partly right?

3. Summarize in one or two sentences Didion's main point about migraine headaches.

4. Decide whether this essay fits more into the rhetorical classification of informative or persuasive. What are the reasons for your decision?

5. How would you describe Didion's word choice? List some adjectives that apply.

6. Reread the closing lines of the essay. Can you understand why this is a suitable conclusion?

7. Didion's essay was written in 1968. Has the care and treatment of migraines improved or changed since then? Do some research on the subject, and write up your findings.

8. Using information in this essay, write a reply to someone who says that migraine victims "bring it on themselves."

9. Write an essay in which you explain, as Didion does, how an apparent misfortune can prove to be beneficial.

HOW FLOWERS CHANGED THE WORLD (p. 308)

LOREN EISELEY

Eiseley's essay is written for a general audience and is notable for its command of language and respect for its subject matter. His word choices help him achieve a sense of wonder about the process of evolution and build credibility when he presents evidence. He approaches the poetic with much of his imagery, reinforcing a sense of awe as he paints bright colors onto the grey canvas of time. The structure of Eiseley's essay is an excellent model for cause and effect papers.

Prereading Journal Idea

In a prereading class discussion, talk about the use of subjective and objective points of view. Ask your students to look for the two points of view when they read this essay and to explain what they are (in their journals).

Read Barry Lopez's "A Wolf in the Heart" (p. 325), and compare it with this essay. Lopez's train of thought continues the evolutionary story set out in Eiseley's essay. Notice that Lopez's viewpoint is strictly subjective and is thus easier to discount. Eiseley's presentation of evidence makes his essay seem more objective.

Ideas for Discussion and Writing

1. Why was the flower an improvement over "its early pine-cone relatives" (¶ 1)? What comparison in paragraph 2 helps you understand this improvement?
2. What kinds of food came about through the development of flowering plants?
3. What was the relationship between the new flowering plants and other plants?
4. What was the relationship between the new flowering plants and animals?
5. Point out other cause-and-effect relationships you can see in the essay.
6. How is Eiseley's essay different from a discussion of the same topic in an earth science textbook? Find words and passages that help prove your point.
7. What does Eiseley think about human evolution?
8. Do you think Eiseley regards human evolution as the final result of the development of flowers?

THE PLOT SICKENS (p. 313)

FANNY HOWE

Howe begins her essay with an intriguing situation: the beginning of an unfinished short story she instructed her college students to finish. We are drawn in by this situation, perhaps thinking about what *we* might write for the assignment. She takes the meaningless, unresolved violence in her students' stories as a symptom of their view of the world--a leap some of your students may question. Howe takes further leaps in her speculation that the replacement of the Establishment, which had a face, with the Economy, which has no face, is the cause behind her students' disaffected world view. Though the essay does take chances, Howe admits that it is a speculative one--she does not present her ideas as facts, as writers such as William F. Buckley and Gore Vidal are prone to do. Your students will probably have strong opinions about whether Howe is right or wrong.

Have each student write down the names of three personal heroes or role models. Write the names on the board with tallies next to names with more than one person listing them. Talk about what kind of people the students chose as heroes, and keep the list on the board while discussing the essay.

Comparative Study

Read Marie Winn's "TV: The Plug-In Drug" in Chapter 11 for another essay that speculates broadly on the reasons for changes in society. Which essay do you find more believable? Why?

Ideas for Discussion and Writing

1. What years does Howe's teaching career span? What is your impression of what happened in American society in those years?
2. In paragraph 4, Howe writes, "No narrative line seems to sustain it [the violence in the students' stories]." What does that sentence mean? Can you think of a movie that this sentence could describe?
3. Did paragraph 7 surprise you? What might you have expected in its place?
4. In what ways is the Economy "a more democratic, open, and pluralistic mechanism than the Establishment ever was" (¶ 11)?
5. Trace the cause and effect reasoning in the essay.
6. Choose one sentence in paragraph 21 that could be identified as the thesis of the essay.
7. Compare the heroes and role models discussed in paragraph 18 with the ones your class listed.
8. Give an example of how rage or outrage becomes "misdirected at powerless people" (¶ 22).

HOW TO TELL TIME BY A CAT'S EYE (p. 318)

DONNA JOHNSON

"How to Tell Time by a Cat's Eye" is a catchily (though misleadingly) titled, lighthearted piece of science writing. It has the straightforward purpose of explaining the thread of scientific truth that is woven into each superstition about the natural world. The structure is a simple one: Johnson presents each superstition and follows it with an explanation. Notice particularly how Johnson inserts expert observations in easily understandable contexts. This essay provides a good break from weightier and more depressing pieces.

Prereading Journal Idea

Do you or people you know have superstitions about animal behavior, like "If your cat sleeps on its head, it's going to rain"? How strongly do people believe in these sayings? Is there any truth to them?

Comparative Study

Compare the tone and style of "How to Tell Time by a Cat's Eye" with Loren Eiseley's "How Flowers Changed the World" (p. 308), another essay that explains natural phenomena.

Ideas for Discussion and Writing

1. Johnson provides the example of the violinists and the toads before she expresses the thesis of the whole article. Find the thesis sentence. Why do you think the writer precedes the thesis with an example?
2. This article concerns both valid and invalid superstitions about nature. What techniques does the writer use to let you know which is which?
3. Johnson uses information from several experts in her article. Underline or highlight her *source introductions*--that is, the places where she introduces the experts and tells what their credentials are.
4. How many sections comprise the body of "How to Tell Time by a Cat's Eye"? Identify common patterns of development among the sections. For example, a bold-faced superstitious sentence begins each section.
5. Johnson's article appeared in the magazine *National Wildlife*. What other magazines might publish this story? What type of audience would enjoy the article?
6. Write about superstitions that you or members of your family or neighborhood have held. Frequently these superstitions have to do with success or bad luck in sports, performances, weather, or work. Do the superstitions have any validity? How did these superstitions develop?

A WOLF IN THE HEART (p. 325)

BARRY LOPEZ

Lopez's essay argues by example that the majority of people have lost touch with their animal past. He devotes the bulk of his essay to the often symbiotic behavior of wolves and Native Americans, the customs and viewpoints of Native Americans and how they interrelated with their environment. Lopez provides many examples of the impact that the wolf had on the various tribes living on the continent. As he points out each relationship, he is also explaining the mindset or philosophy of the Native Americans. Their admiration of the social and hunting skills of the animals led them to pattern their own societies after the animals'. Lopez's exploration of Native American philosophy allows the modern reader a critical look at a human society that lived in harmony.

Prereading Journal Idea

In a prereading discussion or journal entry, students might consider their various levels of interaction with nature. Students from farms, students who fish and hunt, students who have pets, and students who live in city apartments will have different experiences of the natural world.

Comparative Study

Read E. M. Forster's "My Wood" (Chap. 1) to get a contrasting relationship between human and nature.

Ideas for Discussion and Writing

1. What are some ways that Indians imitated wolves in their hunting practices?
2. What are some qualities that Indians admired in animals?
3. Look up the words *anthropomorphic* and *animistic*. Do these words describe any practices in your own culture?
4. How did Indians feel about killing wolves? How can you tell?
5. Find ten examples of comparison and contrast structure in the essay.
6. Do you think that mainstream American culture has suffered from its separation from natural processes? How could you go about growing more in touch with nature?
7. Lopez shows how the wolf was fully integrated into the Indians' world view by

80

giving examples from their language, customs, and everyday life. What do our language, customs, and everyday life reflect as our world views?

FAMILY DOCTOR (p. 336)

JOHN MCPHEE

McPhee's informative essay explains the rise, decline, and resurrection of the general M.D. McPhee structures his essay with personal anecdotes to bring the problem to the reader and then objectively argues that the number of general practitioners declined because of technological advances and the corresponding rise of medical specialists. McPhee then explains how the gap was filled by redefining generalists as specialists. He outlines how the state of Maine attracted the much-needed family doctors. McPhee's reassuring essay concludes with a list of requirements that family practitioners must meet to stay qualified.

Prereading Journal Idea

See how many of your students have a family doctor. Did their parents have one as children? Discuss what benefits come from having a general practitioner as a family doctor.

Comparative Study

Compare this essay with Richard Selzer's "Taking the World in for Repairs" (p. 371). In what ways do the authors have the same world view? Compare their views of the goals of modern medicine.

Ideas for Discussion and Writing

1. Have you ever seen one of Norman Rockwell's *Saturday Evening Post* covers? How would you describe them? What is the point of McPhee's reminder of the old magazine covers?
2. What does McPhee think of the way people remember the Great American G. P.? Look up the words *omniscient* and *ubiquitous*.
3. What myths and realities does the author point out in paragraph 2?

81

4. Why have specialists eventually outnumbered generalists?
5. What did the state of Maine do to attract G.P.s?
6. What kind of audience is McPhee trying to reach in this essay? How can you tell?
7. McPhee's essay was written in 1983. How could you find out whether the number of general practitioners (as opposed to specialists) has increased since then? Do you think that McPhee would expect to find that the number of G.P.s has grown?
8. General practice benefitted from being redefined as a *specialty*. Can you think of other examples of improvement (or the opposite) that have come about basically through redefinition of terms?

MEDICINE'S NEW FRONTIER (p. 344)

BILL MOYERS

This is Moyers's personal essay about the quest he engaged in to discover what the mind-body connection can do. Three years of research resulted in a popular Public Broadcasting Service series and a book-length report of his findings, as well as many interviews and shorter works like this one. Moyers has a calm, reasonable tone, giving him credibility that many proponents of mind-body connection lack in their enthusiasm. He also presents his evidence clearly and keeps a personal frame of reference in the introduction and closing. His refusal to reject the wonders of Western medicine also helps him get through to a mainstream audience. It is important to help your students see the ways that he reaches an audience that might be quick to reject non-western ideas.

Prereading Journal Idea

Have you ever meditated or done yoga? Have you ever had acupuncture or acupressure? What do you think of these non-western mental and physical health techniques?

Comparative Study

Read Henry Dreher's "The Healing Power of Confession" in Chapter 8 for another example of the power of the mind-body connection.

1. What was Moyers's original motivation to research the mind-body connection?
2. What is some of the evidence Moyers presents? Do you find it convincing? Why or why not?
3. What techniques do you think Moyers uses to reach an audience that might easily reject non-western ideas of medicine?
4. What is the difference between "healing" and "curing" as explained in paragraph 12?
5. What changes would Moyers like to see in Western medical practices?
6. Why does the author believe we will see these changes made within the next twenty-five years?
7. In the closing, Moyers writes of a state in which "we see all these parts of our being as connected, we come to terms with where we come from, who we are and where we're going." Have you ever experienced this state, or come close to it? Write an essay describing the experience.

SHOOTING AN ELEPHANT (p. 350)

GEORGE ORWELL

Orwell examines his motivation for killing an elephant while serving the British in India. Faced with the generalized expectations of the native Burmese he despises, he must act out the part of an imperialist gun-toting white man. Caught between a hatred of imperial institutions and a more personal disdain for their lazy servants, Orwell is faced with killing an elephant that he would just as soon let live. He is able to justify the killing after viewing the downtrodden corpse of one of the elephant's rages. With this necessary excuse, he is now bound to kill the elephant in order to fulfill the role assigned to him. The graphic details of the dead man and the dying elephant present the reader with the difficult quandary. Orwell's imagery is graphic in order to jar the reader from complacency.

Prereading Journal Idea

Ask students for examples of what they and others have done to avoid looking foolish. Have they avoided certain discussions for fear of appearing stupid? Have they acted more bravely than they really felt to impress others? Have they done things they would usually consider wrong due to social pressure?

Read James Baldwin's "Stranger in the Village" (p. 482), and compare the themes that the two essays have in common.

Ideas for Discussion and Writing

1. Look up the word *parable*. In what way is this story a parable?
2. Reread the first sentence of the essay. What does it imply about being an important person?
3. In paragraph 7, Orwell writes that "when the white man turns tyrant it is his own freedom that he destroys." Explain this statement. Does any tyrant destroy his or her own freedom? Think of other situations where this might be true.
4. The Burmese people were eager to see Orwell shoot the elephant. Why?
5. Do you think that this essay could be called a short story instead? Why or why not?
6. What device does Orwell use to build tension after he shoots the elephant?
7. At the end of the essay, Orwell says he is glad that the elephant had killed someone because it put him "legally in the right" for shooting the animal. What actions today are considered legally right that you, or others, feel are morally wrong?
8. Write an essay about an action you took which led you to some realization about yourself or your situation.
9. Write a essay about a time when you did something you really didn't want to do (or wouldn't normally do) just to avoid being laughed at.

BEATING THE TEST (p. 357)

DAVID OWEN

Most students will enjoy Owen's thorough roast of standardized tests from ETS, though a background in statistics of test construction would help. Owen tries to provide this background by giving examples. Owen's main gripe is that ETS pretends that its tests do more than they really can: they claim actually to measure academic ability rather than achievement and test-wisdom. If this claim were true, no amount of coaching would help a student raise scores. But coaching *does* help, especially when administered by reputable firms like the Princeton Review. You may have students who can contribute personal knowledge of how the coaching works.

Prereading Journal Idea

You have probably taken the ACT or SAT test or both. What do you think affects students' scores on these tests? Do you think the tests are accurate measures of academic ability?

Comparative Study

"Why Pilot Drug Tests Don't Improve Safety Record" by Robert L. Wick (p. 537) is another essay that examines whether tests are really as useful as they seem. In both essays, an underlying principle is that a truly useful evaluation measure would be more complicated and costly than the one currently used.

Ideas for Discussion and Writing

1. What is the difference between ability and achievement?
2. What does the author mean by "the real subject matter of the test . . . is the test itself" (¶ 2)?
3. Why do low-scoring students get the square root of 4 correct when mid-scoring students miss it?
4. What does the example in paragraphs 9-10 demonstrate?
5. What is the "experimental" section for? How might it harm student test-takers?
6. According to paragraph 26, what students are at a disadvantage in taking the SAT?
7. Why do you think colleges keep using tests like the SAT?
8. Write about another test or grading practice that you think is either unfair or inaccurate. Give examples and reasoning, as Owen does.

BEING WEDDED IS NOT ALWAYS BLISS (p. 364)

KATHA POLLITT

Pollitt's essay is a critique of media interpretations of a controversial Harvard-Yale study that noted women over 35 are unlikely to get married. She points out that it is the mass media that are blowing the findings out of proportion as they attempt to prop up old stereotypes. Pollitt presents and interprets her own research, giving alternatives to every simple-minded interpretation offered by the mass media. Her tone is calm and logical. She argues that women in general and professional women in particular do not need to be pressured into marriage. She suggests that many of them are unmarried due to choice, not lack of opportunity. In the first paragraph, Pollitt writes a potential newspaper headline which could serve as the title of her own essay: "Despite Heavy Pressure from Pop Psychologists, Women Still Say No to Men Who Chew With Mouth Open."

Prereading Journal Idea

Ask the women in your class whether they feel or have felt heavy social pressure to marry and have children. Can they peacefully visualize their futures without marriage? Why or why not?

Comparative Study

Read Joan Didion's "In Bed" (p. 304) for a comparable refutation of commonly held beliefs. How do the authors fight back against simple-minded interpretations of statistics?

Ideas for Discussion and Writing

1. What are some of the problems with the Harvard-Yale study, according to Pollitt?
2. What do you think of Pollitt's description of traditional marriage as a situation "in which women barter domestic service and emotional submission for economic support and social recognition" (¶ 16)? What is the "barter" within your own marriage or your parents'?
3. How could our society give support to couples without a stay-at-home partner?
4. Why do you think the media publicized the Harvard-Yale study the way they did? On what other issues do media help shape public opinion?
5. How convincing do you find this essay? Why?
6. What other pressures, besides marriage, do you think prevail upon the average college woman?
7. What pressures prevail upon the average college man?
8. Write an essay refuting a magazine, newspaper, or television report that you feel gives a one-sided or inadequate interpretation of the news.

TAKING THE WORLD IN FOR REPAIRS (p. 371)

RICHARD SELZER

Selzer's earnest tone carries his essay along. He must skirt sentimentality throughout his story because his subject matter is so intensely personal. Selzer reveals that all the volunteer workers are motivated by different reasons: some for the surgical experience, others for a feeling of virtue. Selzer overwhelms the reader with case after case, achieving a sympathetic weariness. In between, Selzer fills in exotic details of the country and recounts the tight teamwork that comes from the medical project. The rich examples and details may renew our faith in doctors.

Prereading Journal Idea

List and explain the various reasons why people do volunteer work.

Comparative Study

Read John McPhee's "Family Doctor" (p. 336), and compare the different views of specialized doctors.

Ideas for Discussion and Writing

1. Why was there a need for INTERPLAST? What is its purpose?
2. What are some of the motivations behind the volunteers for INTERPLAST? Why did Richard Selzer volunteer?
3. In paragraph 2, Selzer writes of "that certain 'sweet arrogance' that belongs to men and women trained to a fare-thee-well in their life's work." What does he mean? Have you ever seen that "sweet arrogance" in anyone?
4. What are some of the conditions the team must work under? What effects do the conditions have on the workers?
5. What does Selzer feel about the patients? Point out passages that let you in on his feelings.
6. Write a short essay explaining how the title reflects the overall theme of the essay.
7. Selzer writes, in paragraph 1, about forging "professional relationships that would endure, would outlast any political differences between countries." Why is this a significant goal? What professions other than medicine could usefully forge such relationships?

WHAT I LEARNED IN SCHOOL TODAY (p. 389)

Scott Shuger

Shuger's essay takes a hard look at one of the insidious problems afflicting the university system: the deliberate attempts to let athletes slide through four years of classes in exchange for sports performance. His first-hand account of one of these classes is a reminder that such action cheats the athlete in the long run and annoys other academically oriented students at the moment. In contrast to the humorous anecdotes showing thick-headed athletes at their most stereotypical, Shuger amasses statistics showing the widespread academic corruption practiced by sports administrators in order to keep good athletes (but poor students) in school. Shuger portrays his classmate athletes as uncouth apes, but when he quotes them, they become even less credible as fully rounded human beings.

Prereading Journal Idea

Discuss the latest scandals in college athletics and/or the solutions that have been attempted.

Comparative Study

Compare Eugene Izzi's "Down and Out in Chicago" (p. 161) with "What I Learned in School Today" in terms of the role of the writer as observer.

Ideas for Discussion and Writing

1. At the time of Shuger's essay, how did the University of Michigan "shield its jock curriculum from public and faculty view" (¶ 4)?
2. What were Shuger's motivations for attending PE 402?
3. Can you justify curricula like the one for athletes at University of Michigan? Do other majors or courses of study lack academic rigor? Why?
4. What could be done to remedy the student athlete problem?
5. How things changed for collegiate athletics since Shuger wrote this essay? Have they improved or gotten worse?
6. Have you ever attended a high school or college class that you thought was a scandal for one reason or another? Write an essay like Shuger's describing the class.

THE USES OF GOSSIP (p. 394)

Deborah Tannen

Many of your students will have seen Deborah Tannen on talk shows or read one of her best-selling books on communication. Tannen takes knowledge gained from scholarly linguistic research and writes it in easily accessible prose. The key to her success is probably that so many of us recognize our own behavior as fitting into the schemes she describes. Certainly, gossip is something that most people both enjoy and abhor. Here Tannen speculates on what gossiping does for us.

Prereading Journal Idea

Do you gossip? Are there different kinds of gossip? Have you ever been hurt by gossip? How?

Comparative Study

Read Robin Lakoff's "You Are What You Say" (p. 515). Do you think that Lakoff would agree with what Tannen says about male and female use of language? Why or why not?

Ideas for Discussion and Writing

1. How do high school girls get status, according to the essay? Do you agree? How do high school boys get status?
2. In what ways does gossip reinforce values?
3. Look up the word *ostracize*. Have you had any experience with ostracism? Do you agree that it is practiced more among girls than boys?
4. How could talking to friends be risky for women? For men?
5. What is the difference between how men and women bond through talk? What are some reasons for the difference, in your opinion?
6. Write about an experience with gossip and relate it to Tannen's ideas.
7. Write about some other social or language difference you perceive between men and women. For example, you might write about friendship, compliment-giving, advice-giving, or telephone habits.

"THIS IS THE END OF THE WORLD": THE BLACK DEATH (p. 399)

BARBARA TUCHMAN

Tuchman begins with the incident that introduced the plague to Europe and goes on with an overview of the difficulties involved in gauging the extent of the disease. Her gruesome account of the body disposal problems and the desolation are enhanced by an objective and dispassionate tone. She uses statistics with examples to bolster her general statements. The accounts of the survivors bring the reader closer to the horror endured by the ancient writers. Her points and conjectures are based on many different accounts: the impressive scholarship of the piece should be stressed.

Prereading Journal Idea

Ask the students whether any have been in a natural disaster or calamity--earthquake, hurricane, epidemic, flood, and so on. Did they see the calamity unifying people in mutual aid or pulling them apart in fear?

Comparative Study

Read "Taking the World in for Repairs" (p. 371), and discuss the contrasting points of view toward medicine and humanity.

Ideas for Discussion and Writing

1. Where did the plague probably first appear?
2. Why were there two different sets of symptoms of plague?
3. Who was at most risk of being infected with the plague? Why?
4. In paragraph 15, Tuchman writes, "the plague was not the kind of calamity that inspired mutual help." Why not? What were some of the social reactions to the disease?
5. How are reactions to the AIDS epidemic similar and different from reactions to the fourteenth-century plague?
6. Why does Tuchman use so many direct quotations from writers of the plague years?
7. Where does Tuchman believe St. John drew from for his depiction of the plague in the Bible?
8. Choose another natural disaster to research and present in writing, using Tuchman's essay as a model.

THE TRUTH ABOUT LYING (p. 409)

JUDITH VIORST

Viorst takes up a thorny issue here--whether or not to tell little white lies. She refuses to make the moral judgment herself, as she explains in the opening. Instead, she presents the readers with plenty of examples in which people do tell lies and asks us to decide for ourselves whether they are right or wrong. You might want to emphasize the form of the essay--classification, in which a large number of items or examples are grouped into meaningful categories.

Prereading Journal Idea

Think about the last lie you remember telling. Would you call it a minor lie? What motivated you to tell it?

Comparative Study

Read Deborah Tannen's "The Uses of Gossip" (p. 394). If you were to classify different types of gossip, using Viorst's format, what might your headings be?

Ideas for Discussion and Writing

1. Identify the four main types of lying that Viorst discusses. How are the divisions between the types signaled? What is another way to signal divisions within an essay?
2. Reread the opening paragraph. What expectations does the introduction create? Does it reflect the type of essay that follows? How?
3. Viorst calls her essay "a series of moral puzzles." Why are they puzzles? What is Viorst's own moral stance on the issue of lying?
4. Who is the intended audience for "The Truth about Lying"? How can you tell? How does Viorst draw the reader into the essay?
5. Although the subject matter is adult, this essay has an eighth-grade readability level. What makes it so easy to read?
6. Write about a lie you have told that you believe is justifiable. Does it fit into one of Viorst's categories? If you prefer, write about a lie that was told to you and how you responded when you discovered its untruth.

7.   Another of Viorst's essays classifies the types of friends she has made. Write an essay classifying either types of friends or types of conversations.

VIOLENCE IN SPORTS (p. 415)

ROBERT YEAGER

Yeager sullies the already tarnished image of professional sports with his chronicle of violence culled from worldwide sports sources. He supports his thesis by a long list of violent incidents. The essay begins with a worried comment from a professional athlete and ends with a rhetorical question from a retired athlete. In between, Yeager cites a variety of theories purporting to explain the rise in sports-related violence.

Prereading Journal Idea

Discuss sports as the major interest--or at least subject of conversation--among males in our culture. Are women as interested in sports as men? Why or why not?

Comparative Study

Read Scott Shuger's "What I Learned in School Today" (p. 389). What unspoken attitudes run through the behavior of the athletes depicted in these essays?

Ideas for Discussion and Writing

1.   In paragraph 1, Yeager says that sports "may be our only religion." In what ways could sports be compared to religion?
2.   Whom does Yeager quote to support his main idea? Why does he use these people as sources?
3.   Would Yeager's article offend hard-core sports fans? How might they respond to his points?
4.   What's wrong with over-aggressiveness winning the game, according to Yeager?
5.   Do you think Yeager is a sports fan himself? Why or why not?
6.   Who is involved in sports violence other than the players themselves?

7. Do you think that "most of us know quite well when an act of needless savagery has been committed" (¶ 14)? Can you as a spectator or as a player know when unnecessary violence is happening in a game? How?
8. Try to answer the essay's final question, asked by Al DeRogatis.
9. Yeager's book (from which this excerpt was taken) was written in 1979. Has the level of violence in sports grown since then? Write an essay in which you update and comment on Yeager's discussion.

Chapter 10

ESTABLISHING CREDIBILITY (p. 421)

To be persuasive, writers and speakers must gain the respect and trust of their readers. A person's character is embodied in his words, and the way this character is perceived by others largely determines how credible the person and her arguments will be perceived. The ancient Greeks called this particular effect *ethos*, and they valued it highly. The little boy who cried "Wolf!" when there was no wolf soon lost his credibility. His ethos was damaged--and people quit listening to him.

How Does a Writer Establish Credibility? (p. 421)

Writers and speakers can build a reputation for being credible or not. Ask students which newscasters and reporters they respect and admire the most. Why? Do they regard the school paper as a credible source? Perhaps you can find some letters to the editor that question the credibility of a story or a reporter; use these to demonstrate the importance of being credible. Or bring in some supermarket tabloids, which are always fun to look at, and read some of the incredible stories. Why are they so clearly incredible? You can also use advertisements and promotional flyers to examine for evidence of credibility (or lack of it).

Other questions to ask: "What are some sources that you do regard as trustworthy and reliable? What about encyclopedias? Do you believe what you read in your textbooks? Why or why not? How do advertisers try to build up their credibility? Are they successful?"

Being Knowledgeable About the Topic (p. 422)

You can establish your credibility first by establishing your credentials for writing about the topic. Show that you have some personal experience with the subject; show that you have thought about the subject carefully and/or have researched it.

Here are some questions for determining whether you can effectively present yourself as knowledgeable enough to write persuasively about a topic:
- Can you provide information from sources other than your own experience?
- What are your sources? How reliable are they?

- Do your sources contradict one another? If so, can you resolve or account for the contradictions?
- Do you have personal experience that relates to the topic? Is it applicable?

These questions will help you to explore your own knowledge and consider your available resources; they will help you see what you have to do to establish your credibility. Perhaps you need to do more research, check some sources, take a new approach, or even find a new topic.

Demonstrating Fairness (p. 423)

Showing respect for other points of view does not necessarily weaken your position. It demonstrates that you are being fair and evenhanded--and thorough--in your approach to the topic.

Here are some questions for exploring ways to demonstrate fairness toward opposing arguments:
- What are the differing points of view on this issue? How can you demonstrate that you are aware of them?
- Do you understand and sympathize with points of view other than your own? How and where can you express this understanding?
- Can you show that you have considered all the evidence carefully, even evidence which does not support your position?

Avoiding Logical Fallacies (p. 424)

We have, somewhat reductively, divided logical fallacies into four types. Students might enjoy bringing in examples of these fallacies from advertising, newspapers, cult publications, and letters from friends and parents.

If you want to review this material quickly, here's an alternative list of recommendations for examining logic and detecting fallacies; they cover the same points that are in the text but in slightly different terms:
1. **Avoid oversimplifying**. Be wary of arguments that offer no middle ground.
2. **Avoid stereotyping**. Stereotypes involve set notions of the way different groups of people behave.
3. **Avoid sweeping or hasty generalizations**. Question easy solutions to

complex problems; provide evidence to support general claims; qualify broad assertions.

4. **Watch for hidden premises**. Analyze conclusions carefully; look for unexpressed assumptions.
5. **Do not dodge the issue.** Refrain from playing on the emotions, prejudices, fears, and ignorance of your readers.
6. **Keep an open mind.** Thinking is your best defense against logical fallacies. Don't make up your mind too quickly; let the facts lead you to a conclusion.

LOGIC PRACTICE (p. 427)

Students will have fun--and little difficulty--analyzing the illogic in these statements, which is most notable in the cause and effect category. The letter writers invoke inappropriate authorities, appeal to fears and emotions, make sweeping generalizations, and reduce complex issues to simple, either/or solutions.

Analyzing Credibility (p. 428)

These two essays present a contrast in tone and approach. It's likely that students will find the first one more persuasive and credible than the second. Kupfer is more conciliatory and takes greater care to address the concerns of readers who might disagree with her. Mainardi is more confrontational, although she shows that she has clearly thought about the topic in some detail. Subject matter and a reader's relevant personal experience (or lack of it) may, of course, have something to do with differing reactions.

You can relate considerations of credibility to the ideas about voice that were raised in Chapter 6. Ask students to think about what kind of people the writers are: "What are your impressions of these authors? How would you describe them? Do you think you would like to get to know either or both of them? How much are you aware of their presence in the writing? What do they say to make themselves seem reasonable and believable? What are their qualifications for writing on these topics?"

If time is short, you can skip one of the selections, or assign both but analyze and discuss only one. If students are keeping journals, ask them to read both essays but write only about the one they found more credible.

Prewriting (p. 435)

Asking students to re-read the essays reinforces the connection between reading and writing. We learn how to write persuasive essays by closely observing what published, professional writers do. The PREWRITING ACTIVITY asks the students to decide which essay they found most persuasive and figure out why. It can be done in groups or as homework. You might alert students to these questions when you assign the readings and ask individuals or groups to be responsible for certain items.

Other relatively short essays that are interesting to analyze for their credibility and persuasiveness are "Drugs" by Gore Vidal (p. 534), "Why I Want a Wife" by Judy Brady (p. 490), "Dear Dads: Save Your Sons" by Christopher Bacorn (p. 479), "Parents Fight to Counter Culture" by Ellen Goodman (p. 501), and "Rock Lyrics and Violence Against Women" by Caryl Rivers (p. 522).

Writing a Persuasive Essay (p. 435)

Every student should find one of the IDEAS FOR WRITING compatible and appealing. You might conduct several five-minute freewritings in class on each of the topics (or on the two or three that each seems most interested in) to help students choose the one they're going to write on. If time permits, discuss the freewritings and let the students inspire each other with thoughts and ideas on each topic.

Rewriting (p. 436)

Students can work in pairs or groups, exchanging papers and making suggestions for enhancing credibility and improving logic. Suggest they use the questions in Chart 10-1, and write out the answers to any that seem appropriate. Some of the easiest material to add in rewriting a persuasive essay is an acknowledgement of other points of view and sentences that demonstrate an awareness of counterarguments. Remind students of the ways in which Fern Kupfer deals with opposing arguments and corrects her readers' probable misconceptions about institutions for retarded people.

Chapter 11

TAKING A STAND (p. 439)

In the first edition of this text, we presented Toulmin's new (well, sort of--new since Aristotle) system of informal argument. But the feedback we received indicated that students were confused by the terminology, so we have gone back to the traditional terms. In fact, we offer here instruction not in argumentation, but in persuasion, since today there seems to be a far greater call for the skills involved in writing persuasively than in presenting formal arguments.

In college, students will again and again be asked to take a position on some issue and defend it--often in writing. They will also be deluged with deceptive language by advertising, government, and various other sources throughout their lives. They need to become sensitive to the connotations of words to enable them to recognize loaded language. They need to understand the pernicious uses of persuasion in order to distinguish the truth from the tripe.
Thus, the material explained in this chapter is important not only for a successful college career but for a successful life after college as well.

What Is Persuasion? (p. 439)

We have simplified classical argumentation to make it serve as a means of organizing a persuasive paper. The first step will produce by far the longest section of the essay--the presentation of your case. The second step, refuting the opposition, may be quite brief (as is the case in Marie Winn's article on the deleterious effects of TV on the family) or fairly long (as is the case in William Styron's scathing denunciation of the tobacco industry, which follows). The third step will vary in length, depending upon whether the opposition has a strong case or not. Winn concedes very little, Styron nothing at all.

We explain in the text itself how we think Winn's persuasive essay follows the three steps.

WORKSHOP ACTIVITY (p. 445)
This assignment asks students to defend television as a benefit to family life--a tough topic for most adults but perhaps easier for young people who are not so jaded. If you have any debaters, they may welcome the chance to try to find evidence to substantiate the less easily defended side of a controversy.
If, however, your class draws a blank on this topic, change it to something on

which they can choose sides, like the distribution of birth control information or condoms in public high schools. Any current controversy will do here.

Besides being longer, Styron's essay is proportioned quite differently from Winn's.

1.   Presentation of case--paragraphs 1 through 4, in which he discusses his personal experience with cigarettes and bronchitis.

2.   Refutation of opposing arguments--paragraphs 5 through 8, in which he brings up the argument of free speech as being the favorite defense of cigarette advertising; then he proceeds to demolish that claim by pointing out that these ads constitute "seduction of the young." The claim that cigarette are no worse than alcohol is a cop out, he says, because cigarettes do nothing to give pleasure except relieve the very craving that the drug in them has created. Alcohol, he argues, is at least a mixed blessing: it provides pleasure when used in moderation, unlike the "bogus pleasure and incalculable harm" of cigarettes.

3.   Concession of points and reinforcement of position--he considers that the tobacco industry has no defense, period, so he concedes no points (readers whose lives do not depend upon tobacco tend to agree). His position is powerfully reinforced through the closing narrative about the tobacco company executive who is obviously dying from the effects of cigarette smoking yet refuses to believe that smoking is harmful.

Writing: Drafting a Persuasive Essay (p. 450)

We have provided a number of writing suggestions here hoping that your students will find one of them appealing. The last one, number 5, is not meant to invite a rehashing of Styron's essay, but a student might be able to follow his general argument while substituting his or her own personal narratives about cigarette smoking. Or, if a student should be bold enough to take up the challenge of first amendment rights as reason enough to continue to allow cigarette advertising, that topic is wide open.

ADDITIONAL READINGS

You may want to assign supplementary reading before you ask your class to write a paper taking a stand on some issue. Here are several suggestions. You will also find more topics for writing following the discussion of these essays in this Instructor's Manual. All appear in the Anthology of Persuasive Writing:

Rewriting: Detecting Loaded Language (p. 452)

This instruction is aimed primarily at making students aware of the way language can be used to manipulate them if they are unable to recognize loaded words. But, at the same time, they will be empowered by knowing how to use strongly connotative language in order to persuade others to accept their point of view. Advertisements are usually full of loaded words. Have your students bring in several examples, or bring in several full-page magazine ads to analyze their use of language--either in groups or as a whole class.

Encourage your students to adopt a permanently questioning attitude, like the "built-in doubter" that Issac Asimov says has served him well as a scientist (in the first essay in the Anthology of Persuasive Writing, p. 469).

REVISING ACTIVITY (p. 453)

After your students have done the word substitutions called for in this exercise, you could go through the last two steps in small groups during class.

Here's another suggestion: if your students are tired of their own essays, you could have them exchange and add stronger language to someone else's writing. Then partners can discuss the effectiveness and accuracy of the changes.

Chapter 12

ACHIEVING UNITY (p. 455)

Of course, you have been encouraging your students to consider unity whenever they write a paper. Certainly, the easiest way to produce a nicely unified piece of writing is to follow a nicely unified plan. Or, it's perfectly possible to turn out a tightly unified essay by outlining the first draft to discover how the ideas fit together, and then revise to rearrange ideas if necessary or add paragraphs to plug gaps in thought if needed.

In this chapter we introduce several additional ways of achieving unity through coherence: using transitional terms, rhetorical questions, echo transitions, and deliberate repetition.

What Is Unity? (p. 455)

This section expands the brief advice we offered in Chapter 3 on coherence. Students should by now be ready to attempt some of the more sophisticated methods that we explain here, and they should also learn to employ the typical transitional terms gracefully and with restraint. Echoes--both between paragraphs and from introduction to conclusion--are the mark of a skilled writer. Advise your students to put a check mark in the margin when they find such echoes in any of their reading. They will learn from observation as well as from practice. Encourage them also to work on echoes and deliberate repetition as part of their revising process. Both techniques require conscious effort; they don't just happen. Even the best of writers have to work to achieve these polished touches.

Looking at Unifying Devices (p. 460)

Your students should by this time have developed good reading habits. They should be regularly underlining, checking, starring, and noting their responses in the margins.

Prewriting (p. 462)

In our "Prewriting" instructions, we ask them to mark all of the transitions they see

101

as they read through Raspberry's essay the second time. We trust that on first reading they may already have underlined a number of key passages and crowded the margins with responses to the author and notes to themselves.

You might want to suggest that they use ink of a different color to distinguish second-reading notations from their initial responses.

PREWRITING ACTIVITY (p. 462)
We would respond to these questions this way:

1. We found the words used 8 times in 15 paragraphs, clearly repetition that produces coherence and continuity.

2. The idea of teenage pregnancy (the focus of the article) appears in both introduction and conclusion, sounding a clear echo and reinforcing the message.

3. "Those numbers" in the opening sentence of paragraph 2 refers directly back to the "numbers" cited in paragraph 1--i.e., the "more than a million" pregnant adolescent girls, 400,000 of whom had abortions, and 600,000 of whom became "unmarried mothers."

4. The rhetorical question "Can anything be done?" lets Raspberry report two possible solutions offered by the National Academy of Sciences. First, he mentions their call for easily available birth control for teenagers and education to encourage them to use it (¶ 4). Then he advocates the second (and for him the more important) means for trying to solve the problem: fostering better self-concepts and instilling hope for future achievements among teenaged girls (¶s 5-11).

5. This is an echo transition, but it echoes an idea, not the actual words. Raspberry mentions "two answers" in the last sentence of paragraph 3; then in paragraph 4, he takes up the first of these answers: "The one [answer] that made the news was. . . . "

6. The "but if" prepares readers for a contrasting idea; the "also" introduces that new idea.

7. He achieves emphasis in several ways here: he sets off a single sentence as a paragraph; the sentence is a fragment; it's also extremely short; and it uses deliberate repetition.

102

8.   The transitional terms "on the one hand" and "on the other hand" allow Raspberry to highlight what he sees as a contradiction in the report by contrasting the two ideas.

9.   This is not a typical rhetorical question--i.e., one that a writer poses and then proceeds to answer.   He seems genuinely to be wondering why this phenomenon occurs, and clearly he wants his readers to wonder about it also. We gave the matter some thought, and one reason that occurs to us is the possibility that this solution (easy access for teens to birth control and encouragement to use it) is a practical one that could actually be implemented, if it were not for strong opposition from some religious groups.   So, the idea has the appeal of a notion that sounds as if it would work.

10.   This "solution" that Raspberry favors (i.e., somehow giving teenage girls positive self-concepts and career aspirations) strikes us as extremely difficult to bring about.   In our culture girls traditionally have been brought up to envision themselves as prospective mothers, to see motherhood almost as their *raison d'etre*.   Our culture also induces feelings of inferiority and helplessness in females.   All of these deeply rooted influences would have to be changed--and should be, of course.

      We think some progress is presently being made in this direction.   But also the problem of poverty would have to be addressed, since poverty engenders feelings of hopelessness and counters positive career aspirations. We stand solidly in favor of attempting to bring about all of these changes, but recognize that such problems are far more easily discussed than solved. Perhaps discussion, though, will prove to be the first step toward bringing about change.

Writing (p. 463)

IDEAS FOR WRITING
      Our suggestions for writing in this section are demanding.   In fact, your students may need help with invention here. We suggest in the text that they do some reading, but they may have difficulty in discovering what to read. It would probably be wise to spend some time in class discussing suitable topics (those that we suggest or similar ones that you and your students may think of).

SUPPLEMENTARY READING
      You may want to have the class read additional essays in the Anthology of Persuasive Writing to provide them with more examples of well unified pieces, and new ideas may catch their interest.   Also, you will find topics for writing in the

103

Instructor's Manual following the discussion of these essays. Here are some suggestions for supplementary readings:

> Christopher Bacorn, "Dear Dads: Save Your Sons" (p. 479)
> Judy Syfers Brady, "Why I Want a Wife" (p. 490)
> Sue Halpern, "Telling the Truth" (p. 503)
> Adam Smith, "Fifty Million Handguns" (p. 525)
> Gore Vidal, "Drugs" (p. 534)

Rewriting (p. 464)

In this section we explain the technique of echoing some element from the introduction in the conclusion. You might want to let each student choose one of his or her earlier essays and revise the opening and closing paragraphs to include an echo. The results of this exercise are usually quite gratifying.

PRACTICING ECHO TRANSITIONS (p. 465)

We ask students here to incorporate an echo from the introduction into the conclusion of the paper they are now working on. Then we encourage them to focus their attention during the revising process on several means of ensuring unity throughout the essay.

You should, of course, as you read the final drafts of these essays, pay particular attention to how well the writers achieve coherence. Be sure to praise them if they produce a pleasing echo or use an effective rhetorical question to achieve transition.

MODELLING REPEATED STRUCTURES (p. 465)

Students often enjoy modelling exercises because this method allows them to stretch their abilities and produce more elegant and sophisticated writing than they normally do. Call their attention to our sample of paragraph modelling so they will realize that they need not reproduce the structure exactly. You might want to allow them to choose their own paragraphs, if they have favorites. Here are other suggestions of writing that is well worth modelling from the Anthology of Expressive Writing:

> Paragraph 9 of Orwell's "A Hanging" (p. 176)
> Paragraph 3 of Faulkner's Nobel Prize speech (p. 149)
> Paragraph 1 of Welty's "The Little Store" (p. 206)
> Paragraph 19 of White's "The Geese" (p. 219)

Be sure to stress the importance of copying the piece precisely, as the copying serves an integral purpose in the pedagogy involved here, a sort of imprinting of the structure of the original in the mind of the one copying.

ANTHOLOGY OF PERSUASIVE ESSAYS

MY BUILT-IN DOUBTER (p. 469)

ISAAC ASIMOV

In this essay Asimov explains the nature of the scientific method; at the same time he defends his apparently contradictory attitude about flying saucers. He explains that a scientist must have a working built-in doubter or otherwise the unfortunate researcher will almost certainly be spending most of a career in theoretical blind alleys. Asimov presents some effective examples to demonstrate why scientific thinking progresses slowly but constantly improves and refines itself. He notes that the foundations of various disciplines (i.e., astronomy, physics, chemistry, biology) have not been overturned in centuries, making it all but impossible for them to be challenged today--simply because too much evidence has been amassed to support the basic premises and concepts of these fields. From this essay, general readers will get a better understanding of how science works.

Prereading Journal Idea

Ask students if they believe in flying saucers: why or why not? Do they think that science fiction writers believe in everything they write about?

Comparative Study

Compare this essay to "Why Pilot Drug Tests Don't Improve Safety Record" (p. 537), especially in the way each author uses evidence and reasoning to make his case.

Ideas for Discussion and Writing

1. How does Asimov explain the fact that he doesn't believe in flying saucers, even though he writes about them?
2. How does Asimov make the transition from talking about flying saucers to the scientific method?
3. What are "titanium oxide," "thulium oxide," and "americium oxide," and why

105

does the author have different reactions to the hypothetical claims about them? Do you need to know what these substances are to understand Asimov's point? What *is* his point?

4. The author says that "doubting is a serious business that requires extensive training to be handled properly." What does he mean?

5. Summarize the theory about atoms that Arrhenius developed (¶s 22-37). Why did his professors doubt him? Why didn't they fail him? How does this case support Asimov's argument about doubt?

6. Asimov says that the "very mechanism of scientific procedure . . . is designed to encourage doubt and to place obstacles in the way of new ideas." Can you give some examples from your own experience and study to support this observation?

7. Explain the analogy that Asimov makes between the scientific method and Darwin's concept of "natural selection" (¶ 55). Is this a helpful analogy?

8. What questions does Asimov ask himself in deciding how much to believe, or doubt, an idea or theory? (¶ 75)

9. Write an essay in which you explain and support Asimov's claim that one person's opinion is not necessarily as good as the next person's (¶ 18).

10. Write an essay that argues for the existence of flying saucers.

DEAR DADS: SAVE YOUR SONS (p. 479)

CHRISTOPHER N. BACORN

As a psychologist, a counselor, and a father, Bacorn is abundantly qualified to comment on the problem of absentee fathers. He begins with a case history, one which he returns to in his conclusion. This brief narrative frames the problem that Bacorn is addressing. He spends most of his essay explaining the extent and the consequences of the problem. Although he does not offer a specific solution, Bacorn clearly thinks that fathers need to spend more time with their children, especially with their sons. He doesn't say exactly why so many fathers shirk their parental responsibilities, but he implies that social values and cultural roles are to blame. Men are not expected, as women are, to be nurturing care-givers; men *are* expected to be successful wage-earners and important members of the community. Bacorn's anger and frustration with the status quo are kept in check in his writing, but these feelings inspire his argument and give it its forcefulness.

Have students do some freewriting or journal writing on their relationship with their fathers. Or consider these questions: what makes a good father? what roles or duties of parenting are expected of a mother but not of a father?

Comparative Study

Compare Bacorn's ideas about fathers with Judy Brady's ideas about wives in "Why I Want a Wife" (p. 490). In what ways are Bacorn's criticisms similar to Brady's?

Ideas for Discussion and Writing

1. Why does Bacorn begin with a specific case history? How does he use this incident to build his argument?
2. Why has Bacorn concluded that "most adolescent boys can't make use of professional counseling"?
3. The subject of this essay is absentee fathers. What's the thesis--that is, what does the author say or claim about absentee fathers?
4. Do you agree that there aren't many fathers who do such things as attend PTA meetings, go to recitals, and take their children to the doctor's office? Why don't they?
5. According to Bacorn, who are the real men in our society? What is he implying about the other men?
6. What solutions does Bacorn offer for the problem he describes?
7. What are Bacorn's feelings about this subject? How can you tell?
8. Write an essay suggesting solutions to the problem of absentee fathers.
9. If you have any evidence from your own experience and observation, refute Bacorn's contentions about fathers.

STRANGER IN THE VILLAGE (p. 482)

JAMES BALDWIN

James Baldwin wrote frequently about the pain and rage of African Americans and of his own search for identity and responsibility in a racially divided world. This

107

essay emphasizes his sense of alienation from the culture and history of white Europeans and white Americans. Baldwin writes about his effort, as a black person, to come to terms with his feelings of exclusion and foreignness. He begins with a personal description of his stay in a mountain village and works toward a generalized discussion of interracial power relationships. The dismal history of the treatment of black people, Baldwin claims, has resulted in a kind of social schizophrenia for white Americans, who cannot live comfortably with African Americans because they do and do not recognize blacks as fully human.

Prereading Journal Idea

Ask students if they have ever been in a situation where they felt like a stranger or a foreigner. "Why did you have this feeling? Can you describe the feeling? What did you do?"

Comparative Study

Read Elizabeth Wong's "The Struggle to Be an All-American Girl" (p. 220), and compare her feelings of being different to those described by Baldwin.

Ideas for Discussion and Writing

1. What impression of the Swiss village does Baldwin convey?
2. In what ways, specifically, was Baldwin a "stranger" in this village?
3. What significant contrasts does Baldwin develop between the villagers and himself?
4. At what point do you realize that Baldwin is writing about more than a Swiss village and his awkward position in it? What broader application of the word *stranger* does Baldwin make?
5. In paragraph 11, Baldwin says that Americans have attempted to make an abstraction of the Negro. What does he mean? To what extent does Baldwin make an abstraction of the white man?
6. According to Baldwin, why was it "impossible for Americans to accept the black man as one of themselves" (¶ 14)?
7. Explain the clash of identities that Baldwin describes in paragraph 16. Do you agree with him?
8. This essay was written forty years ago. What has happened in "the interracial drama" in America since then? Are Baldwin's perceptions and conclusions

about race relations in the U.S. still applicable and valid?
9.   Write an essay in which you explain and respond to the last sentence in the essay: "This world is white no longer, and it will never be white again."

WHY I WANT A WIFE (p. 490)

JUDY SYFERS BRADY

The author says that her own experience, plus discouraging advice from male teachers, inspired her to write this essay, which first appeared as the "Backpage" feature in *Ms.* magazine in December of 1971. It has been widely reprinted and is one of the best-known manifestos of popular feminist writing. Judy Syfers has changed her name to Judy Brady, but her trenchant attack on wifedom remains surprisingly (and unfortunately) relevant. Brady lists the roles of a wife and the many duties that a compliant woman could be forced or induced into assuming. The sentence "I want a wife" is short and childlike, and its repetition suggests that the generalized husband is egocentric and selfish. Brady classifies the duties by paragraph, moving from child care and money to more personal problems of sexual relations. Her exaggeration and omission of positive elements will lead many readers to dismiss her argument as shrill and irrelevant. But her thesis would be greatly weakened if her generalized husband were less demanding. Nonetheless, the essay is carefully organized, and the strong feelings it evokes are quite persuasive to many readers.

Prereading Journal Idea

Ask students how their parents divide up the household duties. Or, if you have married students, ask them how they share the duties of running the house, looking after the children, etc. Is the distribution of work even and fair?

Comparative Study

Read Robin Lakoff's "You Are What You Say" (p. 515). How do these two essays relate? How does language contribute to the roles and stereotypes that guide our thinking and behavior?

1. According to what principles does Brady organize the details of her essay into paragraphs?
2. Think of at least two reasons for the frequent repetition of the words "I want a wife."
3. What kind of person is the "I" in this essay? What kind of person is the wife?
4. Why does Brady avoid calling the wife "she" (repeating the noun *wife* instead of using a pronoun)?
5. Does Brady overstate her case? What effect would a less- demanding imaginary husband have on her thesis?
6. Have things changed since Brady wrote this essay? Do wives still play roles as humble and self-effacing as the one Brady details here? Are men and women freer today to depart from prescribed gender roles?
7. Write an essay entitled "Why I Want a Husband" or "Why I Want a Boyfriend" that defines the stereotyped roles traditionally assigned to men in our society. Or choose another role that you think would fit the ironic approach that Brady uses: "Why I Want a Big Sister," "Why I Want a Roommate," and so forth.
8. Go to your local bookstore and review the text of greeting cards designed for wives, husbands, fathers, or mothers. Putting together the concepts you find, write an essay that defines a wife, husband, mother, or father as imagined by the greeting card industry.

SIN, SUFFER, AND REPENT (p. 493)

DONNA WOOLFOLK CROSS

This essaay is excerpted from Cross's book *Mediaspeak*, in which she maintains that the language of television (which she calls Mediaspeak) "is a way of perceiving reality" and "provides us with our windows on the world." In this excerpt, Cross demonstrates how soap operas present inaccurate portrayals of family life and tries to alert us to some of the potentially harmful effects of these shows. Cross feels that "we seem oddly unaware that much of what we believe to be true derives from television." Although this may be a debatable conclusion, one that assumes most viewers are unable to distinguish between television and real life, the many illustrations she provides in this selection support Cross's specific observations and advance her broader claims about the influence of television.

Prereading Journal Idea

Ask students how many of them watch soap operas. Why? Do television shows like these shape our beliefs and values or merely reflect them?

Comparative Study

Compare Cross's analysis of soap operas with Marie Winn's conclusions about the effects of television ("Television: The Plug-in Drug," p. 440) or with Caryl Rivers's views on the connection between song lyrics and violence against women (p. 522).

Ideas for Discussion and Writing

1. Cross precedes her essay with two epigraphs. Explain how these quotations function.
2. What strategy does Cross employ in her opening to engage the reader and introduce the topic?
3. Are all of Cross's examples actually taken from soap operas? Which ones does she invent? Why does she do that? How would you describe the tone of the invented dialogue?
4. What sources does Cross use to confirm her own observations? Is this corroborating material persuasive?
5. To what audience is Cross addressing her criticisms? How can you tell she's not writing to soap opera fans?
6. In her last paragraph, Cross delineates the "vision of morality and American family life" conveyed by soap operas. Do you consider that vision to be positive or negative?
7. Cross suggests that people who watch these programs accept the soap opera version of family life as real. Do you agree?
8. Why do people find soap operas so appealing? Write an essay in which you explain the appeals.
9. Respond to the claim that soap operas present deceptive and socially detrimental illusions.

PARENTS FIGHT TO COUNTER CULTURE (p. 501)

ELLEN GOODMAN

Goodman's thesis is that "Parents are expected to protect their children from an increasingly hostile environment" (¶ 7). What is new about this responsibility is that it involves working against the prevailing culture. Goodman contends that there has been a "fundamental shift" in the way parents are having to raise their children. Parents used to support cultural values; now they must resist them--and try to get their children to do the same. Her argument centers on the term *counterculture*, which used to mean demonstrations, hippies, and alternative lifestyles. Goodman turns the word into a verb phrase that means opposing or contradicting the dominate culture, which she sees defined by television, movies, and advertising. Part of her case also involves what she sees as the diminishing influence of various institutions (school, church, government) to define and preserve societal values. In Goodman's view, it's all been left to parents, who are pitted against MTV and Madison Avenue. Whether or not this is a fundamentally new role for parents is arguable, but Goodman's thesis is provocative and should stimulate some interesting reactions about the influence of popular culture, particularly from readers who are parents.

Prereading Journal Idea

Ask students to give their opinions about children's television, especially Saturday morning programs. Are they nothing but extended commercials? And if they are, what's the harm?

Comparative Study

Several essays in the persuasive section deal with the influence of popular culture on societal values and could be compared with Goodman's article: "Sin, Suffer, and Repent" by Donna Cross (p. 493); "Rock Lyrics and Violence Against Women" by Caryl Rivers (p. 522); and "Television: The Plug-in Drug" by Marie Winn (p. 440).

Ideas for Discussion and Writing

1. What does "counterculture" mean? How does Goodman re-define this term to fit her argument?
2. What is Goodman's thesis?

3. What source does Goodman cite to support her argument? Is it a credible source?
4. Explain the "fundamental shift" in child-raising that Goodman claims has occurred. Do you agree with claim?
5. Is Goodman advocating censorship? If not, what is she advocating?
6. Is Goodman a parent? How do you know? Does knowing if she's a parent make any difference in the way you evaluate the ideas in this article?
7. What solutions does Goodman offer for parents? Does she imply any? Are there any?
8. Is it more difficult to be a good parent than it used to be? Write an essay in which you answer this question.
9. Write a letter to the editor in response to Goodman's column. You can either support or attack her argument.

TELLING THE TRUTH (p. 503)

SUE HALPERN

In this essay the author uses an extended example to present the argument against parental consent laws for abortion. Halpern doesn't address the argument directly; her presence in the writing is almost nonexistent. Instead she lets the story of Becky Bell's death--and especially the reaction of Bell's parents--carry the argument. Halpern moves back and forth between the events surrounding Becky's death (in the past) and the political activities of Becky's parents (in the present). The Bells, of course, are the perfect opponents of parental consent laws: they're conservative, middle-class parents who never dreamed their teen-age daughter would get pregnant and were confident that if she did, she would not be afraid to come to them. In fact, as Halpern points out, the Bells didn't even know that their state (Indiana) had a parental consent law. In many respects, the Bells are just like a lot of Americans who oppose abortion on demand and support, in theory, laws that require parental consent or parental notification for a teenager to get an abortion.

Prereading Journal Idea

Cite these statistics: more than a million adolescent girls get pregnant in the United States every year (almost 3,000 a day), and some 400,000 of them have abortions. Then ask students what they think our society should do, if anything, about teenage pregnancies.

Compare Halpern's essay to the others that deal with abortion and teen pregnancy: "We Do Abortions Here: A Nurse's Story" by Sallie Tisdale (p. 272) and "Sexual Decisions Based on Values" by William Raspberry (p. 460).

Ideas for Discussion and Writing

1. What is effective about the way Halpern uses the opening two paragraphs to lead into the topic?
2. What is Halpern's position on parental consent laws? Why doesn't she ever express her own opinion directly?
3. Why are the Bells effective at "preaching to the unconverted"? What qualities make them unusual but effective opponents of parental consent laws?
4. How do politicians respond to the Bells?
5. Where does Halpern introduce the statistics about teenage pregnancies in the U. S.? How does she link the numbers to Becky Bell? What is implied by this juxtaposition?
6. Why does Halpern include the information about Mary Moe and Judge Mitchell (¶s 14-17)? What point is she making?
7. Why didn't Becky tell her parents? What probably caused her death?
8. Comment on the ending. Why is it effective?
9. What can be done to prevent teenage pregnancies? Write an essay in which you offer some recommendations. Direct you ideas to a particular audience: school officials, parents, teenage girls, teenage boys, politicians, or some other specific, relevant group.

I HAVE A DREAM (p. 511)

MARTIN LUTHER KING, JR.

This famous speech is noted not only for the effect it had capping the rhetoric of the civil rights movement but also for its perfectly paced eloquence. King's background as a preacher served him in good stead as he came to the forefront of the movement. This piece illustrates some of the major devices common to good speeches: cadence, conviction, imagery, and repetition. The attending crowd was already convinced; they were a friendly audience. King consequently chose emotional appeals over closely reasoned ones. His memorable analogy of the bad check (¶ 4) is the only attempt at persuasion based on reason. Logic and reasoning don't have much effect on prejudice anyway; emotional pleas for justice may be the best tools to fight the irrationality of racism.

Prereading Journal Idea

Discuss the differences between written essays and speeches. Ask what students would do to some of their own essays if they had to give them as speeches.

Comparative Study

Compare King's rhetoric to William Faulkner's in his speech "On Receiving the Nobel Prize" (p. 149). How are these two speeches similar in approach and purpose?

Ideas for Discussion and Writing

1. What audience was Dr. King trying to persuade in his speech? How can you tell? What is his main point?
2. Why does he begin with the somewhat arachic "Five score years ago" instead of simply saying "One hundred years ago"?
3. Look at King's word choice in paragraph 2: what does he achieve by using the words "crippled," "manacles," and "chains"?
4. Explain the metaphor of the "promissory note" and the "bad check" in paragraph 4. Why is it effective?
5. What does King mean by the "marvelous new militancy which has engulfed the Negro community" (¶ 6)? How does this point relate to King's philosophy of nonviolence?
6. If you did not know of Dr. King's Christian ministry, would you guess that he was a preacher from reading this speech? What strong biblical influences can you detect?
7. According to King, how has the government and the power structure of the country failed minorities?
8. To what degree do you think religion played a part in the civil rights movement? Write an essay linking your religious beliefs to your ideas about social injustice.
9. Has Dr. King's dream been fulfilled? Write an essay in which you cite examples to answer this question.

YOU ARE WHAT YOU SAY (p. 515)

ROBIN LAKOFF

Most of us assume that English belongs equally to everyone who uses it and that men and women, therefore, speak the same language. But several studies have revealed that female conversational patterns differ markedly from those of males. Science writer John Pfeiffer has reported that analysis of recorded conversations by two University of California sociologists shows that women ask 70 percent of the questions and men make 96 percent of the interruptions (*Science '85*: January/February issue). Although no one theory accounts for all the differences, linguists like Robin Lakoff point to the subtle forces of gender-stereotyping and gender-discrimination as likely explanations. Lakoff asserts that there is a "women's language" that, unlike forceful, emphatic "men's language," is "fuzzy-headed, unassertive," and that women who use it will be "ridiculed for being unable to think clearly, and unable to take part in a serious discussion, and therefore unable to hold a position of power." Some of Lakoff's claims and examples may draw strong reactions from students who are not predisposed to her thesis. You may want to think of additional terms and usages that illustrate some of the differences that Lakoff describes.

Prereading Journal Idea

Ask students if they think that men and women use language in different ways. Is there such a thing as "women's language"?

Comparative Study

Reread the "The Politics of Housework" (p. 431), and compare Patricia Mainardi's descriptions of male-female communication with Lakoff's conclusions about gender differences in language.

Ideas for Discussion and Writing

1. Consider Lakoff's first example of "women's language"--the one about colors (¶ 4). Do you agree with her conclusions on this point? Do men think color distinctions are trivial and leave them to women to worry about? Could there be another explanation?

2. Lakoff calls women "communicative cripples." Give several examples that reveal what she means.
3. Can you explain what a "tag question" is? Do you think that women use tag questions far more frequently than men do?
4. In paragraph 11, Lakoff says that "women's language sounds much more 'polite' than men's" and implies that politeness is associated with weakness. Do you agree with her?
5. Can you think of other parallel terms like *master* and *mistress* that have acquired very different connotations, perhaps even different meanings? Consider *governor* and *governess*, *major* and *majorette*, *poet* and *poetess*. Why is there no such word as *Senatress*?
6. Who is Lakoff's audience? Why did she publish this article in *Ms.* magazine and not in an academic journal devoted to language or sociology?
7. Record several observations of the interactions of men and women in one particular setting: a classroom, a bar, a library, a supermarket, an athletic event, a restaurant. Take careful notes, and write an essay in which you draw conclusions on the way each group uses language.

ROCK LYRICS AND VIOLENCE AGAINST WOMEN (p. 522)

CARYL RIVERS

From its beginnings, rock 'n' roll has provoked strong reactions. In recent years, some people have expressed concern about the messages they hear in rock music and rock videos, contending that songs whose lyrics refer to satanism, Nazism, drugs, sex, and sadistic violence have a damaging impact on young listeners. The response of the multimillion-dollar music industry has been to cry "censorship." In her essay, Caryl Rivers makes it quite clear that she does not advocate censorship, but she does register a forceful protest against rock lyrics that describe--and even promote--violence against women. Her position is that these vivid depictions legitimize and contribute to the "major social problem" of violence against women. She calls for vigorous protest and, especially, for men to speak out on this topic.

Prereading Journal Idea

Ask students if they think people are influenced very much by popular entertainment (music, television, movies).

Comparative Study

Read "Delusions of Safety" (p. 151), and compare Marcia Ann Gillespie's views on violence against women with Rivers's.

Ideas for Discussion and Writing

1. What kind of rock music did Rivers enjoy as a teenager? What distinction does she draw between the lyrics she listened to and the lyrics she is opposed to now?
2. Rivers says that she does not want to be mistaken for a "Mrs. Grundy." What does she mean? Who was Mrs. Grundy?
3. Why is Rivers particularly upset with men and their reaction to this issue?
4. In paragraph 10, Rivers cites examples of young women she has known who were assaulted. Why does she include these examples? What do they add to her case?
5. According to Rivers, how do rock lyrics legitimize violence against women?
6. Rivers does not advocate censorship. What does she want?
7. What are "bluenoses" (¶ 15)? Why does Rivers say that people concerned about this issue should not be labeled "bluenoses"? Do you think she's being defensive?
8. Drawing on lyrics from selected rock songs, write an essay that supports or refutes Rivers's argument.
9. By silently ignoring the violence against women, says Rivers, our culture tacitly condones that violence. What other injustices does our culture permit and encourage? Write an essay about an injustice that you think our society endorses by failing to condemn it.

FIFTY MILLION HANDGUNS (p. 525)

ADAM SMITH

"Adam Smith" is the pseudonym of George Goodman, a Harvard graduate, Rhodes scholar, financial reporter, columnist, lecturer, screenwriter, and co-founder of *New York* magazine. In this essay he weighs the pros and cons of gun control and concludes that some form of regulation is needed to reduce America's penchant for violence. Smith begins his essay by quoting a member of the "gun culture," ostensibly his opposition. But he also emphasizes his own personal experience with

118

guns and his personal interest in gun control legislation. Smith's focus on the typical divisions between the "gun and nongun cultures in our country" is the central concern of his essay. His main point is that this division is unnecessary and counterproductive. Smith grants that registering handguns would probably not prevent criminals from carrying illegal weapons, nor would it have prevented the deaths of Halberstam and Lennon. Nonetheless, he still considers it an important measure. Some readers may have trouble understanding this apparent contradiction, but Smith argues that something must be done and a national gun law would be an effective beginning.

Prereading Journal Idea

Write these two slogans on the board and ask students to respond to them: "Guns don't kill people--people do"; "Guns don't die--people do."

Comparative Study

Contrast Smith's method of arguing for a controversial policy with Gore Vidal's approach ("Drugs," p. 541). Compare Smith's use of concessions and refutation with Caryl Rivers's argumentative strategies ("Rock Lyrics and Violence Against Women," p. 522).

Ideas for Discussion and Writing

1. Do you find Smith's opening strategy effective? What does he accomplish with the quoted conversation?
2. Why does Smith include the recollection of his war experiences (¶ 2)?
3. Do you agree with author Herman Kahn (quoted by Smith in ¶ 3): "Young persons who are given guns go through an immediate maturing experience because they are thereby given a genuine and significant responsibility"? Would the same hold true if these young people were given cars or beer or a credit card?
4. At the end of paragraph 6, Smith concedes that the murders of Michael Halberstam and John Lennon "might not have been deterred even by severe gun restrictions." Why, then, does he bother to mention these notorious murders?
5. In paragraphs 8 and 11, Smith presents the standard arguments for and against gun control. How do the arguments "against" differ in nature from the arguments "for"? How does Smith use these impersonal arguments to introduce his own views which follow?

6. Do you think we have any chance of accomplishing the "hard work" that Smith suggests in the last sentence of paragraph 21? If so, how? If not, why not?
7. How persuasive are Smith's arguments that other societies are far safer than ours because their citizens are not armed with handguns?
8. Smith makes a distinction between handguns and what he calls "long guns." Write a brief essay in which you defend--or attack--the validity of this distinction.
9. Respond to and explain H. Rap Brown's remark "Violence is as American as apple pie" (¶ 16).

DEATH IN THE OPEN (p. 531)

LEWIS THOMAS

Thomas's thesis is that everything dies, and that includes us. But with so many animals dying all around us, Thomas wonders why it is that we see so few of their dead bodies out in the open. He notes the high number of insects that should be dropping all over us and then compares them to the human population and the statistical certainty that we are all dying on a fixed schedule. Thomas argues that we should come to grips with the fact of our mortality in order to be less surprised when it happens to us. He avoids mentioning scavenging animals that cart off the remains of the dead and dying. He probably omits such observations because they would not help us deal with thoughts of our own decaying death--and thus do not serve Thomas's conclusion.

Prereading Journal Idea

Ask students if they have thought about their own death and what their feelings are towards it.

Comparative Study

Compare this examination of death with the one that Barbara Tuchman presents in " 'This Is the End of the World': The Black Death" (p. 399).

1.   How does Thomas structure his essay?
2.   What does Thomas mean when he says that "we know about it [death] as a kind of abstraction"?
3.   Why don't we see more dead animals around? Has Thomas left any possible explanations out of his essay?
4.   Why does Thomas refer to the huge number of insects that are in the air (¶ 5)? What's his point in citing this statistic?
5.   What commonly held views of death is Thomas trying to discredit? Do you agree with the attitudes he expresses in the last paragraph?
6.   Look up the word *synchrony*, and explain why Thomas chose this term.
7.   Is there "some comfort . . . in the information that we all go down together, in the best of company"? Write an essay in which you respond to Thomas's point about the commonness of death.
8.   Write an essay in which you examine some social custom or belief relating to death and argue for or against the value of such a belief or custom.

DRUGS (p. 534)

GORE VIDAL

Written in 1970, this essay addresses a problem that continues to worsen with each passing year. Vidal's radical solution--legalization of all drugs--and his charge that the government was responsible for the deaths of some New York drug users (¶ 10) will probably draw spirited reactions from some students. But as government programs to combat drugs remain ineffective, an increasing number of social scientists, medical professionals, and politicians are urging serious consideration of just the kind of solution recommended in this essay. Vidal assumes an almost combative approach, daring the reader to react strongly to his charges. He also writes with great confidence and directness.

Prereading Journal Idea

Ask students if they agree with the idea that people have the right to do what they want with their own lives as long as they don't interfere with the rights of others. Does this include the right to take drugs or commit suicide?

Compare Gore Vidal's handling of a controversial issue with the approach taken by Adam Smith ("Fifty Million Handguns," p. 525). How do the essays differ in tone and strategy?

Ideas for Discussion and Writing

1. What is the effect of the opening sentence? How would you describe its tone?
2. According to Vidal, why is it unlikely that our drug laws will be eased?
3. How readily do you accept Vidal's argument that "the bureaucratic machine has a vested interested" in keeping drugs illegal (¶s 10, 11, 12)? What evidence does Vidal present to support his claim? How would refute it?
4. Where does Vidal anticipate and try to neutralize opposing arguments? How effective are his attempts?
5. Does Vidal seem credible? How does he try to establish his credibility? What does he say to reduce or challenge his credibility?
6. This essay was written more than two decades ago. Are the views expressed in it still valid and timely?
7. Vidal claims that the Bill of Rights has become "unacceptable to a majority of high school graduates" (¶ 4). What does he mean? Do you agree?
8. Write a rebuttal to Vidal's argument, citing current statistics and trends in drug abuse.
9. Write a letter to the editor of your school or community newspaper in which you propose a solution or partial solution to a particular current "drug problem": alcohol, marijuana, cocaine, caffeine, heroin, Valium, nicotine. Be sure to identify exactly which problem you are writing about and to say why you believe your solution will work.

WHY PILOT DRUG TESTS DON'T IMPROVE SAFETY RECORD (p. 537)

ROBERT L. WICK, JR., M.D.

This essay is a classic example of problem-solution argument. The author states the problem, analyzes the deficiencies in the present system, and offers his solution. Actually Wick's statement of the problem is divided into two sub-areas, considered in sequence. First, he demonstrates the problems with the current drug-testing program for pilots, developing his criticisms with a statistical analysis of both the test results and its costs. Then he turns to the issue of alcohol dependence, which he says is more serious than drug use among pilots, and once again explains in detail how inadequate the present approach to this problem is. In the last eight paragraphs, Wick presents his solution. He explains why alcoholism is really no problem in the early stages of dependence and shows that only pilots in the end-stage of alcoholism are dangerous. Wick claims that these people can be identified early and helped--and at far less expense than the cost of present drug-testing program. Wick's careful analyses and thorough explanations make for a very persuasive case.

Prereading Journal Idea

Ask students what they think of on-the-job drug testing. Have any of them ever been tested?

Comparative Study

Compare Wick's carefully structured argument with Adam Smith's more informal approach. How is each method appropriate and effective for its topic and audience?

Ideas for Discussion and Writing

1. What credentials does Wick have for addressing this problem? Where and how does he establish his credibility?
2. What problems does Wick have with the present system of drug testing for pilots? Why does he find it unnecessary and unjustified?
3. Do you find Wick's analysis of the test results convincing (¶ 4)?
4. Wick says that cost-effectiveness "is worth a further look" (¶ 7). Do you agree?
5. Why does Wick say that alcoholism is more serious problem?
6. What is the function of the two questions at the end of paragraph 8? Why is paragraph 14 just one sentence long?
7. What solution does Wick offer for dealing with the problem of alcohol dependence among pilots?
8. Write an essay in which you analyze a current problem, the way Wick does, and offer a solution for it.

PART FIVE

RESEARCHED WRITING

Chapter 13

WRITING A RESEARCH PAPER (p. 545)

Before you begin the chapter, you will probably want to direct your students to the closing section, "Writing a Researched Essay" (p. 588), in which we give two very broad topics. One focuses on a distinctive process (like the writing process of a famous author), and the other focuses on a problem-solution structure. We feel that these two topic areas allow students plenty of freedom to follow their own interests, yet these topics give guidance toward acceptable theses. They also are exemplified by two complete researched essays in the text, one in MLA style and one in APA style.

If your students start thinking in terms of their topics early, the material in the chapter will be more meaningful as they apply it to their own pursuit.

Schedule a class trip to the library early in the unit to determine what reference tools and other resources are available and where they are located. We also like to hold some class hours in the library during the research process so that we can help students on the spot and monitor their library skills.

General Advice

Most students find procrastination a major obstacle when they attempt a research project. We have found that setting a clear schedule with well-defined checkpoints along the way is a necessity. The checkpoints we enforce are these:

A. Bring in topics to discuss and get one of them approved.
B. Have thesis, thesis question, or hypothesis approved.
C. Present preliminary bibliography and some note cards.
D. Present annotated bibliography of five or more sources. The annotation

includes a three or four sentence summary of the source (which may just be one chapter from a book), followed by a sentence that tells what this source will contribute to the student's own essay.

E. Present outline or writing plan and have it approved.
F. Pass open-book quiz on documentation.
G. Bring part of the draft to class for instructor to check format, like source integration and internal documentation.

Keep a record of steps completed, and don't let a student proceed to the next step until the one before it is completed and approved. Each step needs a deadline date, with deadlines spaced close to each other for steps A, B, and C and farther apart for steps D, E, F, and G.

Quiz on Documentation Style

The following worksheet or quiz will help direct your students' attention to some of the features of the MLA and APA documentation styles.

Part A. Write a correctly spaced and punctuated Works Cited (MLA) page using the following information. Then write a correctly spaced and punctuated References (APA) page using the same information.

The third edition of a book named Grammar Is Fun by Oliver M. Fidditch. The book was published by Macmillan Publishing Company in New York, New York, in 1986.

An essay called Springsteen's Special Magic by Carla Mayhem in a collection of essays about rock and roll. The collection, edited by Spiro Agnew, is named Jump On It, Baby. It came out in May 1983, published by Hip Press in New York City. The essay on Springsteen appears on pages 24 through 28.

A magazine article by David Breo entitled "Confronting AIDS," which appeared on April 26, 1987, in Sunday: The Chicago Tribune Magazine, volume 72. The article appeared on pages 15 through 24.

Part B. Fill in the blanks.

Instead of using numbered notes, the MLA style gives the author of the source and the appropriate _____ number within the paper, surrounded by_____.

125

The APA style also uses the author's name but adds the _____ instead of the _____ number. In MLA style, the author's name and the page numbers are separated by a _____. In APA style, the author's name and the year are separated by a _____. The page listing sources is called _____ in MLA style and _____ in APA style, and this page is organized according to _____.

[Answers to Part B: page, parentheses, date, page, space, comma, Works Cited, References, alphabet.]

Chapter 14

A HANDBOOK FOR EDITING (p. 591)

At the beginning of the semester, you should tell your class about this useful resource. Show them how to use the table of contents at the front of the text in order to find the section they need in the Handbook. Tell them that they need to look up rules concerning punctuation and usage in this handy chapter during the revising and editing stages of their writing.

To make sure that they really do understand how to use the Handbook, you might write a few sentences on the board containing errors in punctuation or misplaced modifiers or faulty predication, and ask the students to find the rules for correcting the mistakes--and then, following these rules, eliminate the problems.

Then explain to them that throughout the course, you will expect them to consult this Handbook while writing their final drafts and also in correcting any errors that you have marked on their work. If the same mistake appears repeatedly, you might ask the student to write out the exercise covering that rule in order to help him or her understand the concept.

If a number of students are having difficulty with the same common error, you might even want to use class time to go over the rules with the whole group and perhaps work out an exercise together. Suggested responses for all the exercises follow here.

EXERCISE 14-1 (p. 597)

1. Yankees are considered to be thrifty, careful, and hardworking.
2. Except when the project involves spending their own money, they have the ability to organize and get things done.
    They have the ability to organize and get things done, except when the project involves spending their own money.
3. They often select jobs that require hard work and overcoming obstacles, such as farming or fishing at sea.
4. They tend to take life seriously, especially respecting tradition and authority.

127

5.   Yankees sometimes have little sense of humor, although they might not know it or be willing to admit it.
Although they might not know it or be willing to admit it, yankees sometimes have little sense of humor.

EXERCISE 14-2 (p. 599)

1.   Clyde is constantly revising his essays; thus he turns in fine finished papers.
Clyde is constantly revising his essays. Thus he turns in fine finished papers.
2.   Your analysis is flawed in several ways. Because you need to rewrite it, let's discuss your problems.
Your analysis is flawed in several ways; because you need to rewrite it, let's discuss your problems.
3.   You have written an excellent analysis, Bertha; you should read it to the class.
You have written an excellent analysis. Bertha, you should read it to the class.
4.   Monroe complains that he never understands the stories; yet he only reads them through once, hastily.
Monroe complains that he never understands the stories. Yet he only reads them through once, hastily.
5.   Plot is the main element in this story, as far as I can tell; characterization is scarcely important at all.
Plot is the main element in this story; as far as I can tell, characterization is scarcely important at all.

EXERCISE 14-3 (p. 601)

1.   The characters singing the jingle dance whenever the tone of the song changes.
Whenever the tone changes, the characters who are singing the jingle dance.
2.   Lyrics to country music often involve broken hearts and forgotten dreams.
3.   Using a psychological approach to the modern novel is a way to gain insight.
Using a psychological approach to the modern novel can provide significant insights.
4.   Reflecting their Aztec heritage, Chicano poets describe their culture in their works.
When Chicano poets describe their culture in their works, they are reflecting their Aztec heritage.

5.   Wharton's fiction is becoming more respected as a result of the women's movement.
      One reason Wharton's fiction is becoming more respected has to do with the success of the women's movement.

EXERCISE 14-4 (p. 603)

1.   A ten-ton elephant weighs less than a whale.
2.   Some whales weigh over a hundred tons.
3.   The sperm whale stays under water for half an hour at a time.
4.   Most whales come to the surface more frequently.
5.   The Antarctic Ocean serves as the home for many species of whales.
6.   The icy waters, full of plankton, provide an abundant food supply for these huge creatures.
7.   The stomach of a whale holds a huge amount of food.
8.   A small blue whale eats as many as twenty-four seals.
9.   These giant mammals often playfully leap from the water just for fun.
10.   Their tails align horizontally with their bodies.

EXERCISE 14-5 (p. 605)

Answers will vary here, depending upon how the reader understands the meaning.

1.   The policeman yelled at Walter Mitty. Being publicly rebuked irritated Mitty very much.
      The policeman yelled at Walter Mitty. The helplessness of the little man irritated the officer very much.
2.   It is obvious that my uncle often works in his garden.
      The fact that my uncle often works in his garden is obvious.
3.   Perfectly clear stories can be made obscure by literary critics using abstract words and vague terms.
      Literary critics can obscure perfectly clear stories by using abstract words and vague terms.
4.   You should reread the story and underline key words. These active reading techniques will help you analyze it better.
      Rereading the story and underlining key words will help you analyze it better.
5.   Optimists and pessimists will always be able to find examples of poetry to support their respective points of view.

129

EXERCISE 14-6 (p. 606)

1.   Most feminists will find either choice acceptable, but to be safe, choose "his or her."
2.   Same thing: her, but the safe choice is "his or her."
3.   Its
4.   He or she.
5.   His or her, although we think "they" is fine because the group indicated by "everybody" is clearly plural.

EXERCISE 14-7 (p. 609)

1.   He and the coach need to communicate more effectively.
2.   The team was upset by friction between the coach and him (between me and the coach).
3.   We fans were beginning to be unsettled by it also.
4.   Juan and I are going to talk to the coach.
5.   Juan is just as unhappy as I (am).

EXERCISE 14-8 (p. 610)

I know that we regard doctors as altruistic when they are treating us and avaricious when they are billing us. But I don't think we can understand the end result--high fees--unless we understand the process of selection and even self-selection by which people actually do become doctors.

[While the paragraph could be written in more formal language, using "This writer" instead of "I" and "we," the informality of the surrounding words--for instance, the use of contractions--makes the informal "I" and "we" more appropriate.]

EXERCISE 14-9 (p. 611)

1.   Dudley Randall's shocking images include "a stud, a stump, a butt, a scab, a knob," as he describes the possible victim of mercy killing.
2.   Lopez's essay informs us of a special relationship between Indian tribes and the wolves, while he subtly suggests our own distance from nature.

3. The relationship between the ideal lovers in Donne's poem is illuminated by a comparison between the two legs of a compass, whose interdependence is emphasized.
4. Martin Luther King's prose style is characterized by parallelism; it draws heavily from the fundamentalist sermon style.

EXERCISE 14-10 (p. 613)

1. While I was in college, an infamous course known as Chem 20 was required.
2. Goodman believes that doctors, at heart, are different from the rest of us.
   At heart, Goodman believes that doctors are different from the rest of us.
3. The patients require a good deal of relief from pain and suffering from the doctor.
   Relieving pain and suffering, the doctor gives a good deal to the patients.
4. Reading the essay, we find a new perspective on medical school.
   Reading the essay, one finds. . . .
   The essay reveals to readers a new perspective on medical school.
5. Competing for a good residency, a medical student is likely to find a withering of his or her social life.
   A withering of social life is common among medical students as they compete for a good residency.

EXERCISE 14-11 (p. 614)

1. began
2. woke or awakened or wakened
3. lies or lay
4. risen
5. chosen

EXERCISE 14-12 (p. 615)

1. make
2. lie
3. used

4. talked
5. supposed

131

EXERCISE **14-13** (p. 616)

Many acceptable revisions are possible. Here are our suggestions.

1. Both cable television and the Public Broadcasting System have provided unwanted competition for the networks.
2. Daytime talk shows and evening game shows are still popular and gain a large audience.
3. Many people are renting video cassettes, staying home, and watching these movies.
4. Many network shows feature recycled plots and boring dialogue as well.
5. Most American children watch several hours of mayhem and murder every day on television.

EXERCISE **14-14** (p. 617)

1. In the movies today women are portrayed as grouchy housewives, sneaky troublemakers, or loose floozies.
   In the movies today women are portrayed a being grouchy, sneaky, or immoral.
2. Movies in the late 1930s often showed women as career-minded, spirited, and intelligent.
3. Katherine Hepburn appeared delighted at getting the best of Spencer Tracy and at being the best reporter on the paper.
4. Of course, at the end she married Tracy, dropped her career, and became a satisfied housewife.
5. Today women in movies are terrorized by sociopaths, slashed with knives, or mutilated with chainsaws.